The VOICE-DRIVEN LEADER

The
VOICE-DRIVEN LEADER

How to Hear, Value, and Maximize Every Voice on Your Team

**Jeremie Kubicek
& Steve Cockram**

WILEY

Published by John Wiley & Sons, Inc., Hoboken, New Jersey.
Published simultaneously in Canada.

For general information on our other products and services or for technical support, please contact our Customer Care Department within the United States at (800) 762-2974, outside the United States at (317) 572-3993 or fax (317) 572-4002.

Wiley also publishes its books in a variety of electronic formats. Some content that appears in print may not be available in electronic formats. For more information about Wiley products, visit our web site at www.wiley.com.

Library of Congress Cataloging-in-Publication Data:

ISBN: 9781394150663 (cloth)
ISBN: 9781394150670 (ePub)
ISBN: 9781394150687 (ePDF)

C9781394150663_290825

Printed and bound by CPI Group (UK) Ltd, Croydon, CR0 4YY

Cover Design by Connelly Rader
Author Photos: Courtesy of the Authors

This book is dedicated to every Voice-Driven leader in the world—those who are committed to developing others intentionally, every day. You are the true Liberators.

Thank you for living out the message and multiplying its impact in cities and sectors around the world.

Contents

Introduction

The Missing Playbook for Developing People

"I had no idea I was killing their potential."

The confession came from Michael, a seasoned executive whose team was underperforming despite his best efforts. He'd tried everything he knew: setting clear goals, providing regular feedback, even going on an overnight retreat. Nothing worked.

What Michael discovered next changed everything: His effort wasn't wrong, but his style wasn't effective; he was speaking the wrong language entirely.

Like many leaders, Michael had been developing everyone the way he preferred to be developed. His Pioneer Voice thrived on challenge and direct feedback, so that's what he gave his team. But his Creative team members needed space to explore possibilities. His Guardians needed structure and clarity. His Nurturers needed appreciation before correction.

His style was keeping a lid on his people.

Once Michael learned to speak each team member's development language, performance didn't just improve; it transformed. Team retention went from 60% to 82% in one year. Innovation metrics doubled. And Michael finally built the team he'd always wanted.

This isn't just Michael's story. It's a pattern we've witnessed across thousands of leaders in organizations worldwide.

Let's Face It: Developing People Is Hard

You're sprinting to meet deadlines. Your boss demands results yesterday. Clients grow impatient by the hour. And somehow, in the midst of this chaos, you're expected to transform your team into high performers. No wonder most leaders' default to "just getting the job done" rather than investing in genuine development.

But here's the uncomfortable truth: If you're not developing your people, you're placing a ceiling on your team's potential—and on your own influence as a leader.

Most leaders don't struggle with development because they don't care. They struggle because they're trapped in survival mode:

- They're consumed with keeping the machine running.
- They lack a proven framework for actually growing people.
- They unconsciously lead through their personal style, unaware of the needs of those they're developing.

The consequences? Development becomes sporadic, reactive, or abandoned entirely. Teams stagnate. Top talent disengages. Potential withers on the vine—and leaders wonder why performance isn't improving.

But it doesn't have to be that way.

Leadership Is a Language—Are You Speaking Theirs?

Most leadership development fails for one simple reason: It assumes everyone grows the same way.

They don't.

That's why we created the 5 Voices framework. It decodes the unique Voice of each person on your team—and shows you how to speak their leadership language, not just your own.

Because here's what most leaders miss:

- If you're a **Pioneer**, your bold vision and challenge energize some—but can silence others who process differently.
- If you're a **Connector**, your enthusiasm inspires action—but might skip the structure certain team members desperately need.
- If you're a **Guardian**, you offer consistency—but can overlook relational nuance or miss moments to encourage.
- If you're a **Creative**, your ideas spark possibility—but your team may struggle to translate your vision into practical steps.
- If you're a **Nurturer**, your supportive approach builds trust—yet you might avoid necessary confrontation when it's needed most.

In short: Most leaders speak their native leadership language, expecting everyone to understand. But the best leaders—Voice-Driven leaders—adapt their approach to speak the language others can actually hear.

This approach follows the concept of the *Platinum Rule*—*"Treat others as they want to be treated"*—by Dr. Tony Alessandra and Dr. Michael J. O'Conneor.

Leadership isn't about speaking louder; it's about speaking the right language.

Voice-Driven leadership is what happens when leader adapt their development approach to match each person's learning style, motivation, and maturity. It's not about changing who you are; it's about becoming fluent in the languages your team needs you to speak.

The Development Square: Railroad Tracks for Leadership Growth

Knowing someone's Voice is just the first step. The next question is: Where are they in their development journey?

That question is why the Development Square exists. Think of it as railroad tracks for your leadership—a clear, sequential path that shows exactly where each person needs to go next.

Most leaders struggle because they're trying to build the tracks while the train is moving. They have no map, no clear sequence for developing others. They jump from tactic to tactic, hoping something sticks.

The Development Square eliminates this guesswork. It shows you precisely how to move people from Unconscious Incompetence to Conscious Competence in their roles. It reveals when someone needs more Foundation before Immersion, more Empowerment before Multiplication.

When you combine the 5 Voices with the Development Square, something remarkable happens: You not only speak someone's language, but you also know exactly where they need to go next. You can diagnose their current position and prescribe the right developmental approach.

It's like having both a compass and a map for developing others. The 5 Voices tell you how to communicate effectively (the compass); the Development Square shows you the territory ahead and the sequence of growth (the map).

Together, they transform guesswork into a science—and turn good intentions into real, transformational results.

That's the premise of this book.

This Is Your Playbook, Not Just Another Theory

This isn't a book of abstract leadership advice. It's a practical, field-tested guide.

You'll master a clear system to:

- Precisely diagnose where someone stands in their development journey.
- Adapt your approach based on their Voice and current needs.

- Navigate them through inevitable struggles, including the dreaded Pit of Despair.
- Transform followers into owners—and, ultimately, into developers of others.

You'll also learn to build a people-development ecosystem—where growth becomes your culture's operating system, not just an aspirational value.

This book is about giving you our best so that you can be your best.

Who We Are and Why We Wrote This Book

After decades of leading companies, coaching CEOs, and training leaders across six continents—from Fortune 500 giants to nimble startups—and partnering with nearly 1,000 consultants and coaches along the way, we've witnessed the leadership development crisis up close. It's not theoretical. It's real.

As the founders of GiANT Worldwide, we've discovered a fundamental truth: As the team leader goes, so goes the team. When leaders improve both their performance and their leadership capacity and genuinely fight for the highest good of those they lead, team performance and productivity thrive.

Our life's work centers on the "how" of leadership transformation—the applied leadership learning. We have dedicated our work to making the complicated, simple—to help leaders know what to do so they can become leaders worth following.

We've seen repeatedly that when leaders commit to knowing themselves deeply, understanding the Voice of those they lead, and speaking to others how they prefer rather than defaulting to their own style, everything changes, literally.

We wrote this book because we're tired of watching talented people walk out the door due to poor leadership. We're frustrated seeing well-intentioned leaders repeat the same ineffective development approaches, expecting different results. And we're convinced that what the leadership world needs isn't another theoretical framework; it needs a practical playbook that actually works.

Many of our readers and clients have asked for this level of detail. It's one thing to hear us speak about these concepts, it's another to have a field guide that you can methodically follow for yourselves. That is what this book does.

How This Book Works

This book unfolds in three parts:

Part I: The Development Crisis focuses on why development efforts so often fail—and how the 5 Voices and Development Square provide a better way forward. You will have an opportunity to go through a personal assessment and commit to the journey.

Part II: The Development Journey provides a detailed roadmap through the four stages of the Development Square—Foundation, Immersion, Empowerment, and Multiplication—plus guidance through the critical Pit of Despair and the Green Room.

Part III: Building a Development System explains how to scale your impact by creating an environment where development becomes systemic rather than sporadic.

This is a book for practitioners—leaders who need solutions, not just theories. Dog-ear it. Mark it up. Return to it often.

Whether you're leading a company, managing a team, coaching clients, or raising a family, this playbook will transform how you develop the people in your care.

Because when you become a Voice-Driven leader, you stop managing tasks—and start multiplying potential.

Let's get to work.

PART

I

The Development Crisis

1

Why People Development Typically Fails

And What Happens When It Works

I'm done. I can't do this anymore.

Sophie shut her laptop with a force that made everyone in the open office look up. After three years as a rising star at the marketing agency, she had just emailed her resignation letter.

Her team leader, James, was blindsided. In his mind, Sophie was on track for promotion. She managed the biggest client accounts. She delivered quality work consistently. What could have possibly gone wrong?

Later that afternoon, over coffee at a nearby café, Sophie explained: "I've been doing the exact same work for three years, James. When I ask about development opportunities, you say 'Maybe next quarter when things slow down.' When I propose new ideas, you tell me to 'stick with what works.' I've watched you hire three outside experts rather than develop anyone on our team. I'm not leaving for more money—I'm leaving because I stopped growing here a long time ago."

James drove home that evening with Sophie's words echoing in his mind. He had always prided himself on being a good leader. He praised his team. He gave them autonomy. He protected them from office politics.

But he had confused management with development. And it had just cost him his best employee.

This scenario plays out in organizations every day.

If leaders truly knew how to develop others, would we still see such high levels of burnout, disengagement, and purposelessness in today's workplaces?

Would talented employees constantly feel undervalued and stuck in their roles?

Nearly every leader claims people development is important, but few make it a consistent daily priority. Why? Because without a clear, sustainable system, development is difficult to maintain day after day.

The good news: When leaders genuinely commit to development, transformation occurs:

- People don't just complete tasks; they think strategically.
- Teams don't just exist; they become influential multipliers.
- Organizations don't just hit targets; they create thriving cultures.

The Development Disconnect

Most development efforts don't fail because leaders don't care; they fail because everything else seems more urgent:

- Client demands
- Financial targets
- Daily operational fires

In this constant rush, people development feels like a luxury—something we'll address "when there's time."

Developing people doesn't fail from lack of care; it fails when everything else crowds it out.

But here's the reality: Every meeting, every conversation, every decision is either intentionally growing your people's capability or accidentally reinforcing limitations. Are you multiplying potential or merely managing tasks? Leadership development isn't an event; it's embedded in the very fabric of how you lead. What are your daily actions actually developing in those around you?

Without intentionality, stagnation takes root, and a team brimming with potential quietly underperforms.

Competing Pressures

Most leaders juggle three competing pressures in their daily work:

1. Clients/customers demanding immediate results
2. Their boss expecting strong performance metrics
3. Team members needing help, clarity, and development

Guess which one consistently gets neglected? You guessed it. When development is ignored long enough:

- Turnover increases.
- Morale deteriorates.
- Decision making stalls.
- Top performers disengage.

You might not notice the pattern at first, but the evidence becomes undeniable—you're still shouldering burdens that your team should be carrying. Every day without intentional development creates a double cost: your increasing exhaustion and your team's growing disengagement. The longer you delay building a development system, the heavier both burdens become.

Alex's calendar alert chimed at 6:45 pm: "Call Emma re: quarterly plan."

He sighed, realizing he'd have to reschedule—again—the training conversation with his newest team member. It would be the third time this month.

His day had been consumed by an urgent client escalation, followed by his boss requesting additional data for tomorrow's executive meeting. By the time he'd handled both, Emma's scheduled slot was long gone.

"She'll understand," he thought, typing a quick apology email: "Sorry, I am going to need to push back our session. I need to finish the client presentation and my boss needs an updated report for the executive meeting tomorrow."

Six months later, Alex sat stunned across from HR, reviewing the exit interview results from four departing team members—including Emma.

The feedback pattern was unmistakable: "Great company, but I wasn't growing." "I needed more coaching, but my manager was always putting out fires." "I wanted to develop and help, but that conversation kept getting postponed."

What Alex hadn't realized was how each postponed development conversation sent a message: You're not a priority. The client matters more. The boss matters more. But your growth? That can wait.

Now Alex faced a painful reality: Handling client demands and executive requests had seemed urgent in the moment, but neglecting development had created a far bigger crisis—a talent exodus that no amount of firefighting could fix and a heavier workload on himself, that wasn't sustainable.

The Cost of Stagnation

People can be an asset if you treat them as such. Unfortunately, most leaders view them as liabilities to manage more than assets to invest in.

Many organizations slip into survival mode, focusing entirely on execution under pressure to meet short-term targets and miss the benefits of employees being assets.

Development starts feeling like a luxury—something for when things calm down.

But that calm never arrives.

Instead, long-term consequences silently accumulate:

- Growth stalls—for individuals and organizations.
- Innovation fades as disengaged teams do the minimum.
- Morale, retention, and energy decline.

Leaders spend more time fighting fires than preventing them.
Work gets done—but at mounting, hidden costs.

> 82% of managers are considered "accidental leaders"—promoted for performance, not people development skills.
> —CEB (now Gartner), *Leadership Development Factbook*

> 70% of employees say they haven't mastered the skills they need for their jobs.
> —McKinsey, *Building Workforce Skills at Scale*

Rather than building self-sustaining teams, leaders become linchpins required for every decision.

When everything depends on them, everything slows without them.

This pattern is especially common in performance-driven cultures where development seems too slow, too soft, too difficult to measure.

The irony: Skipping development doesn't save time; it guarantees greater pressure later.

Developing people isn't a distraction from results. It's how you achieve results that last.

The Development Difference

Let's explore what happens when people development actually works.

People development isn't magic or exclusive to elite organizations. It's a system built on consistent, intentional leadership where:

- Managers provide high support alongside high challenge.
- Leaders understand their own tendencies and the Voices of those they lead.
- People align not just on what they do but on why it matters.

The outcomes are transformative:

- Trust strengthens.
- Collaboration deepens.
- Ownership expands.

Development becomes the primary reason people stay.

When Kristen took over the struggling regional sales team, she inherited a group with high turnover, missed targets, and toxic competition.

"The previous leader was brilliant but intimidating," one team member explained. "We were afraid to ask questions or admit we didn't know something."

Instead of focusing solely on the numbers, Kristen started with development. She began with Voice assessments, helping each team member understand their natural communication style and strengths. She established weekly coaching conversations—brief but consistent—structured around both performance and growth.

When challenges arose, she asked questions before giving answers. When team members struggled, she paired high challenge with equally high support.

Six months later, the transformation was evident. Not only had sales increased by 24%, but the team dynamic had fundamentally shifted:

> "I used to dread team meetings," said Marcus, a veteran sales rep. "Now I look forward to them. We actually collaborate instead of competing."

"For the first time in my career, I feel like someone's investing in who I am, not just what I produce," added Taylor, a newer team member.

When a competitor tried to recruit away two top performers with significant salary increases, both declined. Their reason? "I'm growing here. The development I'm getting is worth more than a bigger paycheck somewhere else."

The development difference isn't just measurable in performance; it's evident in retention, innovation, and cultural health.

Leading Development in Results-Driven Cultures

"My boss thinks leadership development is a luxury we can't afford right now."

Sound familiar? Many leaders want to invest in their people but face resistance from senior leadership who see development as a distraction from immediate results.

Here's the paradox: Leaders who prioritize development don't achieve results despite their focus on people; they achieve better results because of it.

This isn't wishful thinking; it's strategy backed by hard evidence. For example, Gallup research shows teams with highly engaged members—a direct outcome of intentional development—are 18% more productive and 22% more profitable.[1]

---

[1] Gallup 2024 Q12 Meta-Analysis; The Powerful Relationship Between Employee Engagement and Team Performance (Gallup, 2020). See gallup.com under "Employee Engagement Meta-Analysis" section.

> *The real question isn't "Should we invest in development?" It's "Can we afford not to?"*

Organizations like Microsoft, Google, and Salesforce don't invest billions in people development because it feels good. They do it because doing so drives measurable outcomes: innovation speed, customer retention, and adaptability in volatile markets.

Not every leader values development. Some actively resist it due to short-term pressure, to protect their egos, or because of previous failed initiatives.

Your Role in Development

If you're reading this, you believe developing people matters, but belief alone changes nothing. Your team doesn't need your inspiration; it needs your action. Your organization doesn't need another leadership quote; it needs your commitment. Future leaders need a genuine system for growth. The same applies at home—you have the opportunity to develop those closest to you.

Development Beyond the Workplace

"Dad, you're not listening again."

David looked up from his phone to see his 14-year-old son Dylan standing in the doorway of his home office, basketball in hand. It was Saturday afternoon, and David had promised they'd shoot hoops together—two hours ago.

"Sorry, buddy. Just need to finish this email," David said, already looking back at his screen. "Maybe tomorrow?"

Dylan's shoulders slumped. "That's what you said last weekend. And the weekend before that."

After his son walked away, David sat motionless, a realization washing over him. As the regional VP for a global manufacturing company, he spent his workdays emphasizing team development. He led workshops on communication. He created personalized growth plans for his direct reports. He preached about the importance of "building leaders."

Yet at home, he was failing to develop the people who mattered most.

That evening, David replayed the words that Dylan had spoken numerous times. He turned off his notifications and pulled out a notebook and started to sketch out what he knew David needed. He needed time for authentic connection and a safe space to process some of his ideas.

The next weekend, instead of another broken promise, David created a new rhythm—two hours of uninterrupted time with each of his children, designed around their unique Voices. For Dylan, it started with basketball but transitioned into conversations about high school and his future—conversations where David asked questions instead of providing answers.

Six months later, the transformation in their relationship was remarkable. Not because David became a perfect parent, but because he became an *intentional* one.

Let's broaden our perspective.

Everything about leadership and development at work applies equally powerfully at home.

As a parent, coach, or mentor, you're developing people— regardless of your title. Your children observe how you lead, listen, and respond to challenges. They learn what's "normal" through the culture you create.

They need time and encouragement. They need safe spaces to process. They need your belief in them. And when that happens, they are open to your help in developing them.

If you've felt overwhelmed trying to balance good parenting with work and life demands, consider this mindset shift:

You don't need all the answers. You just need to remain intentional.

As with your work team, your family thrives when development is personalized.

Your family deserves the same intentional development you bring to your team— perhaps even more.

What's Next: Self-Reflection

The *Voice-Driven Leader* isn't theoretical; it's a personalized playbook for developing each team member in ways they'll actually respond to.

But to do that effectively, you must become someone worth following.

The next chapter invites honest introspection about your intent and engagement with those you lead.

You aren't expected to be perfect, just authentic.

Because great leaders, like those they develop, don't emerge by accident. They grow with intention.

2

How Effective Are You in Developing Others?

Assessing Your Strengths

Before you can take others around the Development Square, you need to know where you stand as a leader. The most effective leaders develop others only after committing to their own growth—facing the truth about themselves with complete honesty and intentional self-awareness.

Think about the oxygen mask on airplanes—you secure your own mask before helping others. Leadership development works the same way. **Your capacity to develop others will reach only as far as your commitment to developing yourself.**

To help you with this concept, we've created the Voice-Driven Leadership Assessment, a practical tool that reveals the habits, mindsets, and behaviors that define healthy leadership.

The purpose of this assessment is to help you understand your reality in developing others and inspire you to become more intentional in your leadership. The journey to becoming a Voice-Driven leader starts with facing your reality—not to judge yourself, but to commit to growing beyond it.

The Voice–Driven Leader

Here's what consistent, Voice-Driven leadership looks like in practice. Read it slowly—and honestly:

> As a team leader, I'm deeply committed to developing people according to their natural Voice. I understand my own leadership tendencies and I adjust based on what each person needs in their stage of development. My team knows I am for them, not just for myself. I build trust, give feedback, and create space for others to grow—even when it's messy or slow. I know when to support, when to challenge, and when to get out of the way. I've established clear expectations and vision and defined what winning looks like for us collectively. Our culture doesn't just produce results; it produces leaders who understand their Voice and can develop others.

Now pause and reflect:

- How much of this feels true for me right now?
- Would my team recognize this version of me?
- Would my boss agree with this assessment of me?
- Do I honestly agree with this assessment of myself?

Table 2.1 Voice-Driven Leadership Assessment

Use the prompts to evaluate your current leadership approach.

Score each statement on a scale of 1 to 10, where:

10 = Fully true of me

1 = Not true at all

1. I am deeply committed to developing people according to their natural Voice. _____
2. I understand my own leadership tendencies and how they impact others. _____
3. I intentionally adjust my leadership style based on the needs and development stage of each individual. _____
4. My team knows that I care about their growth and development—not just about performance or results.
_____
5. I actively build trust, provide meaningful feedback, and create space for others to grow. _____
6. I stay present and supportive even when growth is messy or slower than expected. _____
7. I can discern when to support, when to challenge, and when to step back to let others lead. _____
8. I communicate clear expectations and compelling vision and define what winning looks like. _____
9. I help create a culture that not only delivers results but develops Voice-Driven leaders. _____
10. I regularly seek feedback on my leadership from those above, beside, and below me to continually grow. _____

How to Use This Assessment Effectively

- **Reflect Honestly.** Your assessment isn't about perfection; it's about progress. Don't overthink your answers. Trust your initial response.

- **Identify Your Growth Opportunities.** Any score below a 7 represents an opportunity for growth. Ask yourself: What's holding me back from being more consistent in this area? What would it take to move just one point higher?
- **Invite Feedback.** Ask two or three team members and a trusted peer to rate you using the same questions. Compare their perceptions with yours to close the gap between your intent and your actual impact.
- **Choose One Focus Area.** Rather than trying to improve everywhere at once, select the single area where growth would create the most significant ripple effect for your team.

Why Voice-Driven Leadership Matters

The strongest leaders are intentional developers who understand the power of Voice. They know themselves, read others accurately, and tailor their leadership approach based on what each person needs to grow according to their natural tendencies.

When you practice Voice-Driven leadership assessment regularly, you:

- Develop deeper relational trust with each team member.
- Create clarity and alignment across your team's different Voices.
- Build a team that grows beyond the limitations of your personal leadership style.
- Accelerate development by meeting people where they are.
- Create a culture of psychological safety where all Voices can thrive.

Self-assessment isn't a one-time event; it's a leadership habit. The strongest teams grow from leaders who lead themselves first and understand how to speak to each team member's natural Voice.

Self-awareness is the start. Voice-Driven development is the system. Multiplication is the goal.

What's Next? Understanding the Power of Voice-Based Leadership

You've taken the first step toward becoming a Voice-Driven leader.

Now it's time to understand how your people want to be led through their Voice—and why leading this way changes everything about how you develop them.

In the next chapter, you'll discover how to adapt your leadership style to each of the 5 Voices to become a truly effective Voice-Driven leader. When you lead based on how others are—not just on how you prefer to lead—you unlock exponential growth at every level.

Let's go deeper.

3

Voice-Driven Leadership

Learning the Leadership Languages

People don't grow just because we tell them to. Growth happens when we meet people where they are, speak their language, and guide them in ways that resonate personally.

Think back to the most impactful teacher, coach, or mentor in your life. What made them memorable? Chances are, it wasn't just what they taught; it was how they communicated. They knew how to connect with you. They didn't rely on a one-size-fits-all system. Instead, they translated growth in a way that made sense to you. That's the essence of Voice-Driven leadership.

Great development doesn't come from rigid models. It comes from adapting your approach to fit how someone naturally thinks, communicates, and learns. That's why we created the 5 Voices—a practical framework to help leaders unlock the potential of each person on their team by understanding who they are and how they communicate and want to be communicated to.

In our book *5 Voices: How to Communicate Effectively with Everyone You Lead*,[1] we introduced the five foundational leadership Voices:

1. **Nurturer**
2. **Creative**
3. **Guardian**
4. **Connector**
5. **Pioneer**

Each Voice represents a distinct way of thinking, speaking, and contributing to a team. Everyone leads with one of these Voices—and when you can recognize someone's foundational Voice, you gain insight into what motivates them, how they process information, and what they need to grow.

We are now going to show you how to tailor your leadership and development approach based on the Voice of the person you're leading. Because when you understand how someone is naturally inclined, you can lead them in a way that connects—not just in a way that feels natural to you.

A 5 Voices Summary

Each Voice brings strengths to a team—and each has a growth path that leaders must recognize to coach them well. The next table summarizes the Voices.

---

[1] Kubicek, J. and Cockram, S. (2016). *The 5 Voices: How to Communicate Effectively with Everyone You Lead*. Wiley.

Table 3.1   5 Voices Summary

Voice	Strengths and Contributions	Challenges When Overlooked	Development Focus
Nurturer	Creates safety, supports others, puts team needs first	Often dismissed or overlooked in louder cultures	Needs relational support and gradual confidence building
Creative	Sees future possibilities, innovates, protects long-term vision	Ideas dismissed as impractical or "too idealistic"	Needs freedom to explore and connect ideas to execution
Guardian	Brings structure, protects standards, ensures processes are sound	Seen as resistant to change or too rigid	Needs clarity, consistency, and clear expectations
Connector	Builds relationships, creates energy, rallies people to vision	Seen as scattered or superficial when under stress	Needs interaction, affirmation, and shared purpose
Pioneer	Drives results, casts vision, leads with strategic confidence	Can dominate or move too fast for others	Needs challenge, ownership, and room to execute

We also refer to two key Voices in every person:

The **foundational Voice** is your natural way of seeing and interacting with the world. It's the voice you lead with and, when developed well, it becomes your superpower.

The **nemesis Voice** is the one that is most difficult for you to understand or appreciate. Often, it's the Voice you least relate to—but learning to communicate with your nemesis Voice is a hallmark of mature leadership.

When you understand someone's Voice, you unlock the key to how they grow.

Scan here to find out which of the 5 Voices is your foundational Voice. It is easy and free.

Learning Leadership Is Like Learning a Language

Imagine you're walking the streets of Paris. You step into a neighborhood café, smile at the barista, and say, "Bonjour!" The barista replies in French, and with your best effort, you try to order in their language. Even if your accent is off or your words are clumsy, the barista likely appreciates your attempt. Why? Because you're meeting them in their language—and that effort earns you connection.

Now imagine a different scene. You walk into the same café, and when the barista greets you in French, you respond loudly and slowly in English:

"COFFEE. BLACK. NO SUGAR."

What happens? The barista stiffens. Their warmth fades. You might even get a smaller coffee than usual. Speaking louder didn't help them understand you; it only made them feel disrespected.

The same principle applies to leadership. Development isn't about speaking louder; it's about learning to translate. When we force our own leadership style onto others without adapting to how they're naturally inclined, we create resistance. But when we take the time to speak their development "language," trust grows—and so does their potential.

Leadership, like language, is about connection. And connection starts with understanding.

This is why Voice-Driven leadership is so powerful. The 5 Voices framework gives you a guide to decode how your people learn, what motivates them, and how to unlock their growth—by meeting them in their language, not just your own.

> *Leaders who force their own language create resistance. Leaders who learn the language of their people create results.*

The 5 Voices: Five Distinct Languages of Learning

Every person on your team has a unique way of thinking, communicating, and growing. If you've ever wondered why some team members respond well to direct feedback while others shut down—or why some thrive in structure while others resist it—it's because they speak different "leadership languages." The next graph shows the five distinct languages of learning.

Each Voice sees the world differently. Each one learns differently. And each one responds to development in its own way.

Here's a breakdown showing how these Voices learn best—and what causes them to disengage when development is misaligned.

The Nurturer: The Language of Relational Connection

Nurturers are people-first leaders who value harmony, care deeply about others, and want to be helpful.

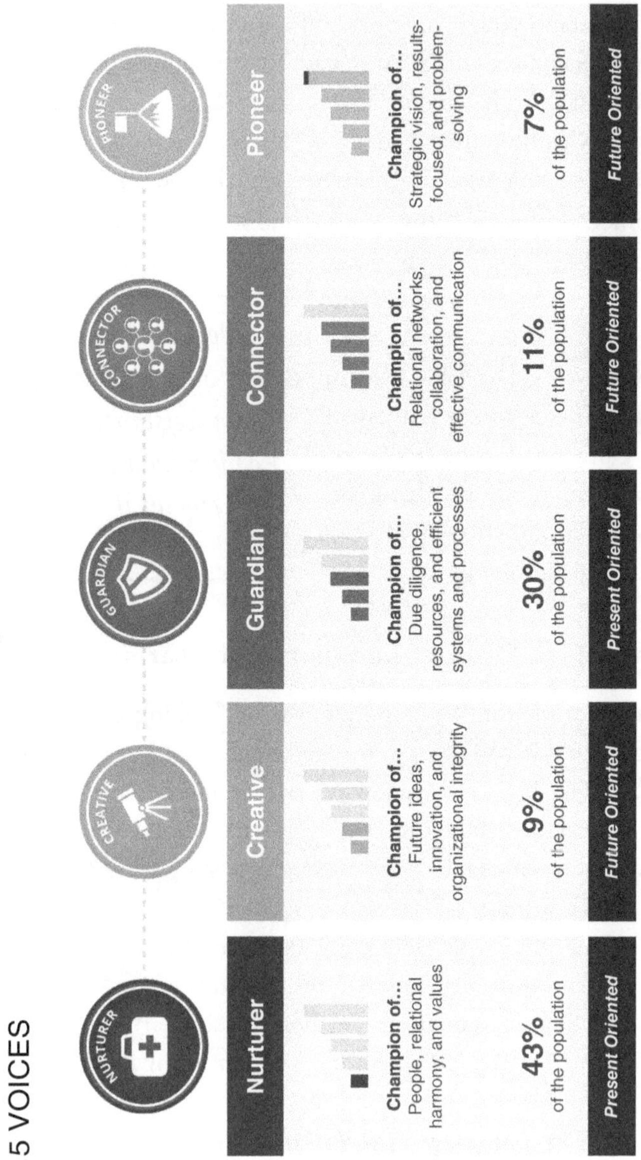
5 VOICES
NURTURER
CREATIVE
GUARDIAN
CONNECTOR
PIONEER
Nurturer
Champion of…
People, relational harmony, and values
43%
of the population
Present Oriented
Creative
Champion of…
Future ideas, innovation, and organizational integrity
9%
of the population
Future Oriented
Guardian
Champion of…
Due diligence, resources, and efficient systems and processes
30%
of the population
Present Oriented
Connector
Champion of…
Relational networks, collaboration, and effective communication
11%
of the population
Future Oriented
Pioneer
Champion of…
Strategic vision, results-focused, and problem-solving
7%
of the population
Future Oriented

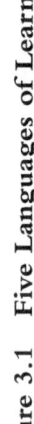

© GiANT Worldwide

Figure 3.1 Five Languages of Learning

Nurturers learn best through:

- Encouragement and emotional safety.
- Step-by-step guidance.
- Relational trust.

They shut down when:

- Feedback feels harsh or impersonal.
- Development is rushed or performance focused.
- Their contributions go unnoticed.

The Paris Café Principle: When you speak Nurturers' language of relational connection, they trust your intentions and open up to growth. But if you push them with hard-edged feedback, they'll feel discouraged and under pressure and can shut down emotionally.

The Creative: The Language of Vision and Possibility

Creatives are big-picture thinkers who are energized by ideas, patterns, and solving complex problems.

Creatives learn best through:

- Conversations about long-term purpose.
- Freedom to explore and experiment.
- Conceptual frameworks with room to adapt.

They disengage when:

- Development is rigid, linear, or overly task focused.
- Their ideas are dismissed too early.
- The "why" is missing.

The Paris Café Principle: If you speak the Creatives' language of vision and possibility, they'll lean into development. But if you dismiss their ideas or force them into strict frameworks, they'll become cynical and disengaged.

The Guardian: The Language of Process and Precision

Guardians thrive on structure, systems, and doing things the right way. They value clarity and consistency.

Guardians learn best through:

- Clear expectations and timelines.
- Practical, repeatable processes.
- Step-by-step coaching with measurable goals.

They resist when:

- The strategy lacks logic or structure.
- Expectations shift constantly.
- Vision isn't grounded in execution.

The Paris Café Principle: Speak the Guardians' language of process and precision, and they'll engage fully. But if you introduce concepts without structure, they'll mentally check out.

The Connector: The Language of Relationships and Opportunities

Connectors naturally build networks, generate enthusiasm, and see social connections others miss.

Connectors learn best through:

- Collaborative, interactive environments.
- Stories and examples they can relate to.
- Seeing how their growth impacts others.

They disengage when:

- Development feels isolated or overly technical.
- They can't see how it connects to people.
- The energy and excitement are missing.

The Paris Café Principle: Speak the Connectors' language of relationships and opportunities, and they'll be fully engaged. But if you focus solely on tasks and metrics, they'll lose motivation.

The Pioneer: The Language of Results and Winning

Pioneers are strategic, competitive, and oriented toward results. They're naturally driven and decisive.

Pioneers learn best through:

- Clear goals and stretch challenges.
- Direct, high-accountability feedback.
- Fast-paced execution environments.

They lose interest when:

- Coaching is overly relational or slow.
- Results aren't measured or recognized.
- They feel held back by indecision.

The Paris Café Principle: Speak the Pioneers' language of results, and they'll rise to the challenge. But if you soften feedback too much or move too slowly, they'll lose respect for the process—and for you.

> *If you want someone to grow, you have to meet them where they are, not where you are.*

The Consequences of Forcing Your Own Language

When leaders default to their own communication style—rather than adapting to the person they're developing—they unintentionally shut down growth.

As we've already shared, it's like walking into a café in Paris and speaking louder English, hoping it will help the French barista understand you. It doesn't work in a café, and it definitely doesn't work in leadership. The louder you push your style, the less it connects.

Here's what misalignment looks like in action:

- A leader delivers blunt feedback to a Nurturer without any relational context, and the Nurturer shuts down emotionally.
- A manager overwhelms a Creative with rigid processes and daily checklists, killing the Creative's enthusiasm and vision.
- A team lead tries to inspire a Guardian with big-picture speeches, leaving the Guardian confused and anxious about next steps.
- A results-driven leader dismisses a Connector's story or idea as irrelevant, causing the Connector to feel unappreciated and disengaged.
- A well-meaning colleague bombards a Pioneer with emotional appeals and slow consensus building, frustrating the Pioneer and slowing their momentum toward results.

The outcome is always the same: frustration, disengagement, and developmental stagnation.

People don't resist development; they resist *misaligned* development.

Understanding Voice Demographics and Their Impact

To develop your people effectively, you need to understand how the distribution of Voices impacts your team dynamics.

Here's what the data tells us:

- **Nurturers** make up 43% of the population. Often present oriented and people focused, typically they are the quietest Voice in the room. They bring deep care, relational sensitivity, and a desire to serve, but they are frequently overlooked or undervalued—especially in fast-paced, results-driven environments.
- **Creatives** make up just 9% of the population. These visionaries thrive in ambiguity and innovation. They are the second quietest Voice. They see patterns others miss and are deeply motivated by potential. Their ideas are often ahead of their time, which means they can be misunderstood or prematurely dismissed.

- **Guardians** account for 30% of the population. These process-driven, detail-oriented thinkers are essential to stability and execution. They tend to ask the tough, clarifying questions and are often the ones who catch mistakes before they become problems.
- **Connectors** represent 11% of the population. Future oriented and naturally energetic, they bring vision, storytelling, and contagious enthusiasm. They love building bridges between people and ideas, and they're often catalysts for momentum.
- **Pioneers** are only 7% of the population, but they are disproportionately represented in executive leadership. As future-oriented, results-driven strategists, they often rise to the top. Their Voice is the loudest, their vision the clearest, and their tolerance for ambiguity and risk is high.

Your Natural Voice and Its Impact on Your Coaching Style

Your natural Voice influences how you develop others.

- If you're a **Nurturer**, you probably lead with empathy—coaching others by supporting their well-being, listening deeply, and protecting relational harmony.
- If you're a **Creative**, you may coach by helping others imagine new possibilities—guiding them to see long-term vision, align with values, and pursue innovation.
- If you're a **Guardian**, you may focus heavily on process and structure—coaching others to follow best practices, reduce risk, and deliver with precision.
- If you're a **Connector**, you likely coach through encouragement and inspiration—motivating people by painting a compelling picture of what's possible and rallying them with energy.
- If you're a **Pioneer**, you may naturally challenge your team toward performance—pushing them to think strategically, move fast, and deliver results.

> *Leadership isn't about who speaks first; it's about who listens best.*

Your natural coaching style works well for people who share your Voice but may miss the mark with those who are naturally inclined differently. When you understand Voice distribution and learn to lead people in their Voice, not yours, you unlock a new level of influence, engagement, and growth.

A Real-World Voice Mismatch

Dan was a high-achieving sales manager with a clear formula for success: Set the bar high, move fast, and never let up. He believed performance came from pressure and that the best way to grow a team was to push people out of their comfort zones.

Dan was successful—but he wasn't a Voice-Driven leader. He led everyone the same way, assuming what worked for him would work for others.

That's when things started unraveling.

Kate had been one of his top performers for two years. She was loyal, consistent, and known for her ability to build lasting relationships with clients. But lately something had shifted. Her energy had dropped. Her results had declined. And Dan couldn't figure out why.

"I don't get it," he said in a team meeting debrief. "Kate used to crush it. Now she looks like she's mailing it in."

What Dan didn't understand was this: Kate represented the largest Voice in the workforce—the Nurturer, which makes up 43% of the population, with the majority being female. Nurturers thrive in environments built on trust, collaboration, and relational connection. They don't respond to pressure the same way Pioneers do. In fact, high-pressure environments without relational support tend to drain them.

Dan hadn't considered this. He didn't know her foundational Voice, and, more important, he didn't stop to ask. Instead of adjusting his coaching, he doubled down on challenge, deadlines, and performance metrics—thinking more intensity would solve the problem.

But to Kate, it didn't feel like a challenge; it felt like criticism. It felt like she was failing. She later told a colleague that she didn't feel like she belonged on the team any longer. She shared how she felt like she's a number, like nothing she did was enough."

The problem wasn't Kate. It was Dan's approach.

Had he understood the demographics of his team—how Nurturers learn, grow, and stay motivated—he would have approached Kate differently. He would have led with connection before correction. He would have linked her performance to client impact. He would have helped her see that her presence mattered as much as her numbers.

But Dan wasn't trained to lead that way. He wasn't a Voice-Driven leader yet.

This story is not uncommon. Many leaders—especially those with louder Voices—unintentionally lead in a way that works for a small percentage of the team. But when they fail to recognize the Voices around them, especially the Nurturer's, which is 43% of the population, their influence will tend to slip.

The good news? The problem is fixable.

Voice-Driven Leadership in Practice

Just as leaders have different coaching styles, team members have different ways they prefer to learn. The key to development isn't just content; its delivery customized to the person in front of you. The next table is a quick reference guide to Voice-based coaching.

If you want your people to grow, don't just raise the bar; adjust your approach.

How to Become a Voice-Driven Leader

You don't need to overhaul your entire leadership style to become more effective. You just need to get more intentional about how you communicate—and coach—based on the Voice of the person you're leading.

Table 3.2   Quick Reference Guide for Voice-Based Coaching

Voice	Best Learning Style	What Doesn't Work
Nurturer	Learns best through relational connection, encouragement, and gradual confidence building	Struggles with overly aggressive challenges, high-pressure environments, and harsh feedback
Creative	Thrives with freedom to brainstorm, explore, and connect ideas to a bigger picture	Disengages with rigid processes, micromanagement, or dismissive responses to their ideas
Guardian	Prefers structure, clarity, and logical steps toward mastery	Gets frustrated by vague direction, changing strategies, or lack of clear expectations
Connector	Learns best in high-energy, interactive, and collaborative environments	Tunes out during monotonous, overly detailed training or solo assignments
Pioneer	Thrives with fast-paced, challenge-driven learning and clear outcomes	Struggles with slow, repetitive instruction or emotional feedback lacking clear direction

The goal is to shift from leading based on your preferences to developing based on their needs. These three steps can help you become a Voice-Driven leader.

Step 1: Learn to Recognize Voices in Real Time

Start by paying attention to how your team speaks, asks questions, and engages with others—especially under pressure or during decision making. The next table lists the common language and behavior of the different Voices.

In moments of pressure or ambiguity, people default to their Voice orientation:

- Nurturers pause to protect relationships.
- Creatives brainstorm better possibilities.
- Guardians slow things down to reduce risk.

People will speak their Voice; you just have to learn to listen.

- Connectors rally people around a compelling vision.
- Pioneers charge ahead toward measurable results.

Step 2: Adjust Your Approach Based on Their Voice

Once you begin to notice patterns, start tailoring your coaching approach to match their Voice.

- **Nurturers** need trust. Remember to lead with empathy and encouragement before bringing challenge.
- **Creatives** value exploration. Give them space to think, ideate, and connect new ideas.
- **Guardians** crave structure. Give them clarity, process, documentation, and defined expectations.
- **Connectors** thrive on energy. Make development collaborative, dynamic, and relational.
- **Pioneers** want challenges. Raise the bar with them, cast an aspirational vision, and track measurable progress.

Table 3.3   Common Language and Behavior of the Different Voices

Voice	Common Language and Behavior in Meetings
Nurturer	"How will this affect the team?"/"Will people feel supported?"
Creative	"What if we did it differently?"/"There's a better way to solve this."
Guardian	"What's the process?"/"Has this been tested?"
Connector	"Who do we need to involve?"/"This could be huge!"
Pioneer	"What's the goal?"/"Let's move faster and win."

Step 3: Track What Works

After every coaching or development moment, take a quick pause and reflect:

- What landed?
- What missed?
- How did they respond, visibly or emotionally?

Over time, you'll start to see patterns. Those patterns will help you lead with greater precision and less friction.

Leadership isn't about pushing harder; it's about listening better and adjusting faster.

Taking Action

Understanding the Voices is one thing. Leading with them is another. Put your knowledge into action this week.

- **Identify Your Default Style.** How do you tend to lead? Do you naturally challenge, support, clarify, brainstorm, or connect?
- **Observe Your Team's Reactions.** Pick two people. Pay attention to how they respond to your coaching. Do they engage, hesitate, or go quiet? That's real-time feedback.

- **Adapt to One Voice.** Choose one person. Match your next development conversation to how they're naturally oriented.
  - Nurturer? Start with trust.
  - Creative? Cast vision.
  - Guardian? Bring structure.
  - Connector? Bring energy.
  - Pioneer? Raise the bar.
- **Note the Shift.** Afterward, reflect: What changed? Did they respond well? Did engagement improve? Was the conversation easier?

Most of you reading this book have been leading for a while. And we get it—changing how you lead isn't always comfortable. We've been refining our own leadership styles for years. But what we're asking is simple:

Be open to the possibility that there's a better, more effective way to lead.

Einstein famously said, "Insanity is doing the same thing over and over again and expecting different results."

If your current approach is exhausting you—or leaving your team disengaged—maybe it's time to try something new.

You now understand how Voice-Driven leadership works. The only question is:

Are you ready to lead this way?

4

Committing to Lead

Choosing to Make Development a Lifestyle

The conference room buzzed with energy as 20 leaders filled their notebooks with insights from their annual leadership retreat. Nathan sat in the front row; his Pioneer Voice energized by the possibilities ahead.

"This is exactly what we need," he thought, scribbling another action item. "These tools will transform my team."

As the workshop concluded, Nathan approached the facilitator.

"This has been transformational," he said. "I can't wait to implement the Support-Challenge Matrix with my team."

The facilitator smiled knowingly. "That's great to hear. But can I ask you something, Nathan? What's your plan for Monday morning?"

Nathan looked confused. "Monday?"

"Yes, Monday at 9 am when 17 urgent emails show up, your boss needs the quarterly report, and your team is looking to you for direction. What happens to becoming a liberating leader then?"

Nathan hesitated. "Well, I'll have to handle the urgent things first, but then—"

"And there's the challenge," the facilitator interrupted gently. "Becoming a leader worth following isn't about what you do when things are calm. It's about your nonnegotiable when everything is on fire."

The facilitator continued. "Remember what we discussed about knowing yourself to lead yourself? Your Pioneer Voice gives you vision and drive, but without intentional rhythms, you'll likely rush ahead without bringing others with you."

Nathan nodded, recognizing his natural tendency.

"Try this," the facilitator suggested. "Each morning, before you do anything else, ask yourself: 'What is the one leadership action I will commit to today to develop one of my employees?' Make that your nonnegotiable, no matter what fires arise."

Six months later, Nathan emailed the facilitator with an update. The daily commitment had transformed his leadership. Although his colleagues from the workshop had reverted to old patterns within weeks, Nathan had created intentional rhythms that changed everything.

His team now spoke a common language. They understood each other's Voices and communicated more effectively because of it. Most important, Nathan wasn't the only leader anymore—he was developing leaders throughout his team.

The Commitment Gap

Most people want to be great leaders. But very few commit to the daily actions that make it happen.

The difference between aspirational and committed leadership is simple:

Aspirational leaders talk about what the organization needs. Committed leaders actually build what they need.

Leadership isn't something you "fit in when you can." It's something you prioritize—especially when things get busy. Without commitment, growth becomes occasional at

> *A leader's impact isn't built on intentions; it's built on daily commitments.*

best. And when the pressure rises, development is usually the first thing to go.

The Three Dimensions of Leadership

Leadership isn't just about making decisions or managing people; it's about growing in three core areas:

1. **Personal Leadership.** Knowing yourself to lead yourself
2. **Relational Leadership.** Knowing others to lead others
3. **Professional Leadership.** Knowing your role and mastering it

Most leaders are naturally strong in one or two areas. But without all three, your influence and effectiveness eventually will stall. Here is why.

- Some leaders are highly skilled in their craft but lack relational intelligence.
- Others build strong relationships but struggle with execution.
- Some are deeply self-aware but fail to lead or inspire those around them.

True leadership requires intentional growth in all three dimensions.

Personal Leadership: Knowing Yourself to Lead Yourself

Before you can lead anyone else effectively, you have to lead yourself. Doing that starts with self-awareness, emotional intelligence, and personal discipline. Leaders who lack personal leadership often struggle with inconsistency, blind spots, or reactive behavior that erodes trust over time. Here are some key questions you can ask yourself to see how self-aware you are:

- Do I understand how my personality and tendencies impact others?
- Am I aware of my emotional triggers and how they shape my decisions?
- Do I live by clear values that guide my leadership?
- Am I consistently investing in my personal growth?

Strengthening your personal leadership is vital to your entire leadership. If you want to strengthen your personal leadership, consider these areas:

- **Know Your Voice.** Use the 5 Voices to identify your natural leadership style and blind spots.
- **Grow in Emotional Intelligence.** Recognize your stress behaviors and learn how to self-regulate under pressure.
- **Build Daily Habits.** Start your mornings with intention, track your progress, and stay accountable.
- **Seek Feedback.** Ask trusted peers or mentors for honest insight into how you lead.

Jeremie's Note: For me, personal leadership meant confronting some unhelpful tendencies—like being defensive or exaggerating to make a point. I learned how to catch those reactions, reframe them, and show up differently. Over time, this gave others more permission to grow, because they saw me doing the same.

Are you ready to commit to knowing yourself so you can lead yourself well?

Relational Leadership: Knowing Others to Lead Others

Great leaders don't just focus on their own growth; they prioritize understanding and investing in the people around them. Relational leadership is about building trust, listening well, and leading each person based on how they naturally communicate and process information.

People don't follow titles. They follow leaders who get them. Here are some key questions you can ask yourself to review your relational leadership:

- Do I know what motivates—and discourages—each team member?
- Am I adapting my leadership based on personality and experience level?
- Do I give regular, meaningful feedback and encouragement?
- Do people feel seen, heard, and valued when I lead?

To strengthen your relational leadership, consider these areas:

- **Know Your People.** Learn their 5 Voices, communication styles, and stress responses.
- **Customize Your Leadership.** Speak to each person in the language that resonates.
- **Build Trust Through Consistency.** Follow through, show empathy, and stay approachable.
- **Coach Consistently.** Don't wait for a crisis. Make development a weekly rhythm.

Real-World Example. One team leader we worked with was frustrated by her team's low engagement—until she began using the 5 Voices. The issue was relational more than professional. Once she understood each person's Voice, communication style, and motivation, everything changed. She built trust, improved morale, and performance took off. She even received cards sharing how thankful team members were for her focus on building relationships.

Reflection to Consider. "Am I intentional about knowing others and leading them in the way they need to be led?"

Professional Leadership: Knowing Your Role and Being the Best at It

Personal and relational leadership build trust, but professional leadership earns respect. This is where your competence, consistency, and execution set the tone for your team.

You can be well liked and self-aware, but if you don't deliver results, your leadership won't last. Here are some key questions to ask yourself about your professional leadership:

- Do I have the skills and expertise required to lead in my role?
- Am I continually sharpening my craft and staying ahead of the curve?
- Do I model the level of excellence I expect from others?
- Am I known for clarity, consistency, and follow-through?

To strengthen your professional leadership, consider these areas:

- **Master Your Craft.** Stay sharp through learning, reflection, and mentorship.
- **Set Clear Expectations.** Make sure your team knows what good looks like.
- **Model Excellence.** Be the example of discipline, quality, and reliability.
- **Measure What Matters.** Use data and feedback to continuously improve.

Real-World Example. A high-potential manager was well liked by his peers but wasn't taken seriously by executives. Why? Because he was average in his role. After focusing on professional leadership—tightening his systems, refining his thinking, and consistently delivering results—he gained credibility and was quickly promoted.

Reflection to Consider. "Do I bring excellence to my role, and am I raising the standard for my team?"

The Power of Integrating All Three Dimensions

Strong leaders don't just specialize in one area; they build capacity across all three dimensions: personal, relational, and professional. That's what makes them stand out.

Many leaders lean heavily into one strength while neglecting the others.

- Some are self-aware and emotionally intelligent, but they struggle to execute.
- Others deliver results and hit goals, but their team doesn't feel seen or valued.
- Some are highly relational but lack the clarity or confidence to lead decisively.

When one dimension is missing, leadership falters. The best leaders grow in all three dimensions. Reflect on these questions to help you improve in your overall leadership:

- Where are you strongest: personal, relational, or professional leadership?
- Where do you feel the most tension or gaps right now?
- How would your team describe your leadership in each of these areas?

By identifying your strengths and growth areas, you can begin developing a more balanced, impactful leadership presence—one that earns trust, delivers results, and builds people.

The Levels of Team Leadership: Who Develops You and Whom You Develop

Leadership doesn't happen in isolation. At every level of an organization, leaders face different challenges—not just in executing their roles, but in receiving and providing development.

Too often, leaders assume development flows only downward. But the best leaders commit to being developed while also developing others. Growth should move in all directions—upward, downward, and laterally.

Let's break down the four key leadership levels, their primary development relationships, and their unique challenges.

CEO

CEOs are responsible for vision and culture building.

Who Develops Them:
- Board of directors
- Executive coaches
- Peer networks (e.g., YPO, Masterminds)

Whom They Develop:
- The executive team
- Senior leaders
- Key specialists

Leadership Challenges. Executive leaders must cast a compelling vision while also ensuring it gets executed effectively. They are constantly balancing the competing needs of employees, customers, and investors, all while navigating uncertainty and leading through change. Ultimately, their challenge is to build a legacy that endures beyond their own tenure.

Executives must actively pursue development because no one is directly overseeing them. The best leaders seek feedback, coaching, and learning from peers and advisors to keep growing. Their influence shapes the entire organization—both its strategy and its leadership pipeline.

Example. A Fortune 500 CEO facing stagnation joined a peer mastermind group. After learning how others developed leaders internally, he launched an executive coaching initiative. One year later, the company had promoted five high-potential leaders into key roles, fueling new momentum.

Senior Leaders and Executive Teams

Senior leaders and executive teams are responsible for strategic operations and shaping culture.

Who Develops Them:
- CEO or C-suite executives
- Executive coaches
- Cross-functional peer leaders

Whom They Develop:
- Directors and department heads
- Emerging high-potential leaders

Leadership Challenges. Senior leaders are responsible for translating the organization's vision into clear, actionable strategies. They must manage both upward—aligning with executive expectations—and downward, ensuring their teams are executing effectively. A key part of their role is preventing departmental silos by fostering cross-functional collaboration. Additionally, they are tasked with identifying and developing the next generation of executive leaders.

Development Focus. Senior leaders play a critical role in scaling leadership across the business. They translate big-picture goals into actionable plans while mentoring the next tier of leadership.

Example. A chief people officer noticed departmental misalignment. She launched a monthly executive roundtable to foster collaboration between department heads, improving both alignment and morale across the board.

Directors and Midlevel Leaders

Directors and midlevel leaders are responsible for executing strategy.

Who Develops Them:

- Senior leaders
- Internal leadership programs
- Peer collaboration

Whom They Develop:

- Frontline managers
- High-potential individual contributors

Leadership Challenges. Directors are constantly balancing strategic goals with the demands of day-to-day execution. They are responsible for managing cross-functional projects that require alignment across multiple teams. A key focus is developing first-time managers, helping them transition from individual contributors into effective leaders. Directors also play a critical role in communicating priorities clearly, both up to senior leadership and down to their teams.

Development Focus. This layer of leadership is where strategy meets reality. Directors must coach their teams, manage operations, and ensure their people are growing while executing at a high level.

Example. A director of product began regular coaching sessions with team leads, using 5 Voices as a foundation. The result? Faster team alignment and a noticeable uptick in project delivery speed and quality.

Frontline Managers and Supervisors

Frontline managers and supervisors are responsible for hands-on supervision.

Who Develops Them:

- Directors and department heads
- Formal leadership training
- Peer mentorship

Whom They Develop:

- Individual contributors
- Emerging leaders

Leadership Challenges. Frontline leaders face the challenge of transitioning from being a peer to becoming a manager, which can be both relationally and professionally complex. They must work to build trust and credibility with their teams, especially when managing former peers. At the same time, they are responsible for balancing the demands of daily performance with the ongoing development of their people. One of their most important tasks is learning to give clear, actionable feedback that drives growth without damaging morale.

Development Focus. Frontline leaders have the biggest impact on employee engagement and retention. Their ability to coach, communicate, and inspire directly affects team performance.

Example. A frontline manager in logistics created a buddy system where experienced team members mentored new hires. Onboarding improved, turnover dropped, and morale skyrocketed.

Development Flows in Every Direction

Most leaders default to downward development, investing only in their teams. But the best leaders grow in three directions.

Direction	What It Looks Like
Upward	Seeking feedback, mentorship, and strategic input
Downward	Coaching and developing direct reports
Lateral (Peer)	Collaborating across functions and learning from others

The best leaders develop in all directions.

Intentional Development in the World of Sports

Some of the best examples of leadership development don't come from boardrooms; they come from locker rooms. In professional sports, success isn't just about talent. It's about development.

Coaches don't assume players will figure it out. They build intentional systems—practices, drills, film study, feedback loops—all designed to bring out each athlete's full potential. The parallels to organizational leadership are undeniable.

Case Study: Gregg Popovich and the San Antonio Spurs

Gregg Popovich, the retired legendary head coach of the San Antonio Spurs, is widely regarded as one of the greatest team developers in sports history. Over his 27-year NBA tenure, he built not just championship-winning teams but a sustainable culture of excellence that outlasted individual stars.

What made Popovich different? He treated leadership development as a core part of the game plan.

Here's how:

- **Clear Expectations from Day 1.** Whether it was a rookie or a veteran, every player knew exactly what was expected of them. Success wasn't a mystery; it was modeled, coached, and reinforced.
- **Personalized Coaching.** Popovich didn't use a one-size-fits-all approach. He tailored his leadership based on each player's personality and mindset. Some needed encouragement. Others responded to the challenge. He knew the difference—and adjusted accordingly.
- **A Culture of Mutual Development.** Players were expected to develop themselves—and each other. Veteran leaders mentored younger teammates. Leadership wasn't positional; it was cultural. Everyone owned it.

As a result of Popovich's efforts:

- The Spurs became the most consistent and respected franchise in the NBA.
- Dozens of players went on to become coaches, general managers, or mentors in other organizations.
- Popovich's leadership legacy continued long after key players retired.

What Business Can Learn from Sports

While business and sports may operate in different arenas, the principles of development are strikingly similar. The best sports teams develop talent through structure, coaching, and repetition—and the best organizations do the same.

Here's how leadership development compares across both fields:

- **Clear Expectations**
  In Sports. Playbooks, roles, and game plans are defined early so everyone knows what success looks like.
  In Business. Job roles, key performance indicators, and success metrics are clearly outlined to guide performance and development.
- **Personalized Coaching**
  In Sports. Coaches adjust based on a player's temperament, learning style, and position.
  In Business. Great leaders adapt their coaching based on each team member's Voice and stage of development.
- **Practice and Repetition**
  In Sports. Athletes engage in daily drills, film study, and situational training to improve performance.
  In Business. Employees grow through ongoing training, project reps, simulations, and structured debriefs.

- **Feedback Loops**

    In Sports. Game reviews and real-time corrections help players improve with every performance.

    In Business. One-on-ones, coaching sessions, and regular performance feedback reinforce learning and accelerate growth.

- **Team Culture**

    In Sports. Winning is a shared mindset. Teams focus not just on individual stats but on collective success.

    In Business. Healthy teams build cultures where collaboration is intentional, trust is cultivated, and leadership is modeled daily.

- **Mentorship**

    In Sports. Veterans mentor rookies, passing down wisdom, mindset, and habits that create consistency.

    In Business. Experienced leaders must intentionally invest in developing the next generation of leaders.

Winning teams don't just recruit talent, they develop it.

Why Leadership Commitment Matters

Most people want to be great leaders, but very few are truly committed to doing what it takes.

Great leaders don't just have good intentions; they take daily, intentional actions to develop their people. Leadership isn't something you "get around to" when time allows. Without commitment, development becomes inconsistent. And when pressure rises, it's often the first thing to go.

Leadership growth isn't an accident; it's the result of daily decisions made with discipline and purpose.

The Three Levels of Leadership Commitment

Every leader falls into one of three categories. The difference isn't talent; it's mindset. The next table explains the levels of commitment.

Table 4.1   Three Levels of Leadership Commitment

Level	Mindset	Impact on Team
Passive Leader	"I'll develop people when I have time."	Growth is inconsistent. Teams drift without direction.
Reactive Leader	"I develop people when there's a problem."	Growth happens under pressure. Morale and trust suffer.
Committed Leader	"I make development part of my daily leadership."	Growth is intentional. Teams thrive and take ownership.

Where Are You Right Now?

Think about your last 30 days as a leader. Have you been passive, reactive, or committed in your development approach?

Take a moment to reflect and rate yourself (1–10, 10 as the highest) on these statements:

1. I am committed to making my teammates better. _____
2. I am more focused on their growth than my own recognition._____
3. I consistently invest time in developing my team. _____
4. I have the mindset and margin to serve and support others._____
5. My team knows what to do, why it matters, and how to grow.___
6. I genuinely enjoy leading this team. _____

Challenge: If any score is below a 7, identify one tangible action you can take to raise it.

What Committed Leaders Do Differently

The best leaders take these actions to be leaders worth following:

- **Assess Their Current Approach.** They know whether they're leading passively, reactively, or with intention.

- **Define Clear Expectations.** They communicate what leadership looks like and what's expected at every level.
- **Build a Development Roadmap.** They provide a clear path for growth, tailored to each team member.
- **Create a Development Culture.** They embed leadership development into the rhythm of work—not as an extra task, but as part of how things get done.

Leadership commitment isn't about being perfect; it's about showing up, stepping up, and building a culture where growth becomes the norm.

Are you ready to become that kind of leader?

If so, you're now prepared to take the next step in your leadership journey. Throughout this chapter, we've explored the three dimensions of leadership, examined how development flows across different organizational levels, and highlighted what committed leaders do differently.

The foundation is set. You understand what leadership commitment looks like and why it matters. Now it's time to put these principles into action.

In the next chapter, we introduce one of the most powerful leadership development tools we've ever created: the Developing Others tool. When paired with the 5 Voices framework you've already learned, it becomes a game changer that will equip you to develop every person on your team with clarity, intention, and impact.

Your commitment to becoming a leader worth following has brought you this far. The path ahead is where transformation truly begins—not just for you, but for everyone you lead.

The Development Journey

5

Understanding the Development Square

Mastering the Art of Leadership Development

"Every day I come in here wondering if today's the day I'll be exposed as a fraud."

Marcus had been on Sarah's team for three months. Despite his impressive resume and initial enthusiasm, his performance was declining. Projects were late. Emails went unanswered. In their one-on-ones, he seemed distant and defensive.

When Sarah finally created space for a real conversation, Marcus's admission stunned her.

"I thought I'd pick things up quickly," he continued, "but nothing was explained. You gave me access to files, introduced me to the team, and then...nothing. I've been trying to figure everything out on my own, and I'm drowning."

Sarah felt a pang of recognition. She'd been promoted for being a high performer, not for her ability to develop others. She'd thrown Marcus into the deep end with no guidance, expecting him to swim as naturally as she did.

"But why didn't you say something sooner?" she asked.

"Because everyone else seems to know what they're doing," Marcus replied. "I didn't want to be the only one asking for help."

Sarah realized she'd failed Marcus—not because she lacked expertise, but because she had no system for development. She had skipped crucial steps, leaving him to navigate blindly when he needed clear direction and support.

This scenario plays out in organizations everywhere. Talented people struggle not because they lack potential but because their leaders lack a structured approach to development.

This issue is what we have been attempting to solve.

We help leaders to not just manage tasks but build people. They understand that developing others isn't about trial and error or blind delegation. It's an intentional process that, when done correctly, transforms hesitant beginners into confident, capable leaders.

The key to unlocking this transformation is the 5 Voices + Development Square, a simple but powerful framework that maps out the four predictable stages every person goes through when learning a new skill.

The Development Square: A Visual Framework

The Development Square (Figure 5.1) maps the journey from novice to master through four distinct quadrants. Each quadrant represents a stage of development characterized by different levels of competence and confidence, with specific leadership approaches needed at each stage.

DEVELOPING PEOPLE

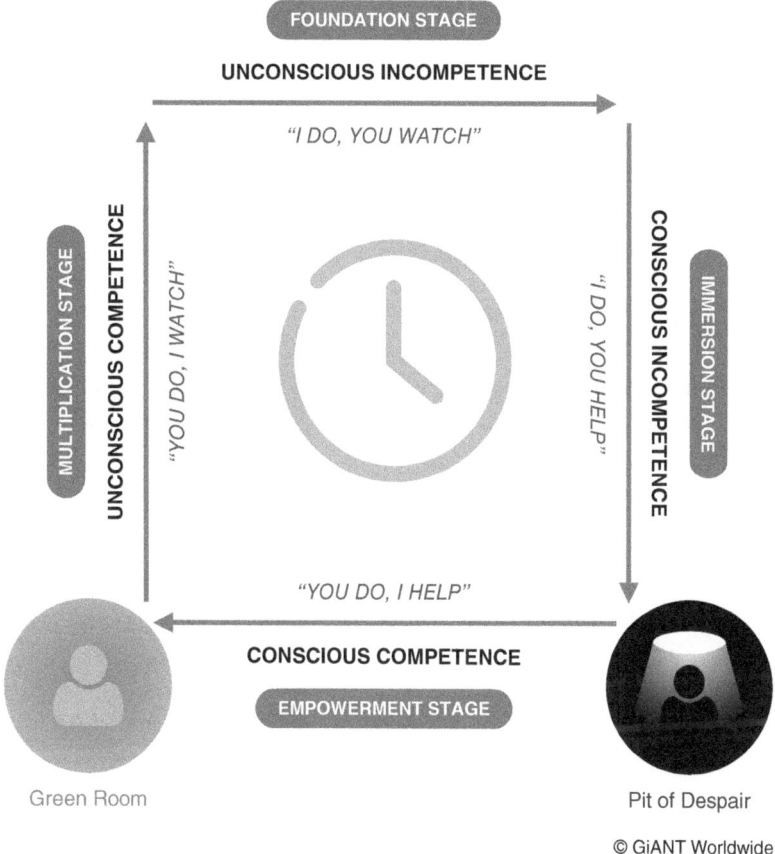

FOUNDATION STAGE

UNCONSCIOUS INCOMPETENCE

"I DO, YOU WATCH"

MULTIPLICATION STAGE

UNCONSCIOUS COMPETENCE

"YOU DO, I WATCH"

"I DO, YOU HELP"

CONSCIOUS INCOMPETENCE

IMMERSION STAGE

"YOU DO, I HELP"

CONSCIOUS COMPETENCE

EMPOWERMENT STAGE

Green Room

Pit of Despair

© GiANT Worldwide

Source Credit: A. Maslow, Gordon Training International

Figure 5.1 Development Square

The progression through the four stages follows a clockwise path:

Foundation Stage (top left): —Unconscious Incompetence— "I Do, You Watch." High initial confidence but low competence; the beginner doesn't yet know what they don't know.

Immersion Stage (bottom left): —Conscious Incompetence— "I Do, You Help." Both confidence and competence are low; reality hits as learners recognize how much they don't know.

Pit of Despair: Between Stages 2 and 3 lies the critical juncture where many learners get stuck. Confidence reaches its lowest point as they fully grasp the gap between their current abilities and mastery. How leaders respond here determines whether someone pushes through to growth or retreats into disengagement.

Empowerment Stage (bottom right): —Conscious Competence— "You Do, I Help." Competence grows but confidence may still be developing; learners can perform the task with effort.

Green Room: Between Stages 3 and 4 exists a comfortable plateau where competent performers may linger. They've mastered their role but haven't yet taken the step to multiply by developing others. Leaders must challenge this comfort to promote true leadership multiplication.

Multiplication Stage (top right): Unconscious Competence— "You Do, I Watch." Both confidence and competence are high; mastery is achieved, and the person can now develop others.

This framework provides a structured approach to development, ensuring your people progress through each necessary stage without getting stuck or skipping crucial growth opportunities.

The best part? When applied correctly, the Development Square eliminates dependency, prevents burnout, and accelerates leadership multiplication.

Whether you're training a new hire, mentoring a high-potential leader, or preparing someone to take on greater responsibility, this model will help you guide them through the process with clarity, confidence, and impact.

Why the Development Square Matters

Imagine a world-class athlete stepping onto the field with no training, no coach, and no understanding of the game. No matter how naturally talented they are, they'll struggle. Without guidance, structure, and intentional progression, they'll make mistakes, lose confidence, and risk walking away altogether.

The same thing happens in leadership development.

Far too often, leaders assume that talented people will "figure it out." They provide minimal training, expecting team members to pick things up on their own. When mistakes happen, they either jump in to fix everything (creating dependency) or grow frustrated that the person isn't performing as expected (leading to disengagement).

The Development Square eliminates these problems by providing a step-by-step roadmap to skill mastery, ensuring that growth happens in the right order, at the right pace, with the right balance of support and challenge.

The Four Stages of Development

The Development Square is built on a natural learning progression that every person experiences when acquiring a new skill. It follows a four-stage journey from complete inexperience to effortless mastery.

Skipping a stage creates frustration, slows development, and undermines confidence. But when leaders guide people through each step, they accelerate growth while ensuring long-term ownership and independence.

The Foundation Stage—Unconscious Incompetence—"I Do, You Watch"

The Foundation Stage is where the journey begins. Learners don't yet know what they don't know. There's usually a sense of excitement—maybe even overconfidence—because learners have not yet experienced the complexity of the task.

What's Happening in This Stage. Learners are observing, absorbing, and forming their first impressions. They feel capable, but it's mostly false confidence rooted in enthusiasm, not skill.

Leader's Role in This Stage. Demonstrate the tasks step by step, narrate your thinking by explaining not just what you're doing but why, and invite reflection with questions like "What did you notice?" or "Why do you think I made that choice?"

Example. A sales leader invites a new hire to sit in on a client discovery call. After the meeting, they debrief by asking what stood out from the meeting, how they might have responded differently, and why certain objections were handled in specific ways, transforming passive watching into engaged learning.

Indicators Employees Are in the Foundation Stage. They ask basic definitional questions, have little or no experience with the task, express confidence despite lack of experience, speak in generalities about how they would approach the task, and rely heavily on transferable skills from other domains.

Common Mistakes Leaders Make in the Foundation Stage. Leaders often overwhelm learners with too much information at once, fail to explain the "why" behind actions, rush through demonstrations to "get back to work," assume prior knowledge where none exists, and neglect to check for understanding before moving forward.

Recognizing When Employees Are Ready to Move to the Immersion Stage. They're ready when they ask insightful questions about the process, can accurately describe key steps back to you, express interest in trying parts of the task, and demonstrate basic understanding of principles.

But then reality sets in. . .

The Immersion Stage—Conscious Incompetence— "I Do, You Help"

The Immersion Stage is where reality hits. Learners begin to see how much they don't know. Confidence drops. Frustration rises. They're helping now—but struggling.

What's Happening in This Stage. The excitement wears off. Learners begin making mistakes. Some feel exposed. For high performers used to success, this is uncomfortable territory.

Leader's Role in This Stage. Let learners participate in a low-risk environment, offer feedback in real time, and normalize the struggle by saying things like "This part of the process is hard for everyone at first."

Example in Action. Alex, a Pioneer Voice type who naturally moves quickly, is learning financial analysis, and his leader, knowing Alex's tendency to rush forward with confidence, intentionally slows down the process, helps him build the analysis with guided support, and points out small errors as teaching moments rather than failures.

Indicators Employees Are in the Immersion Stage. Employees attempt tasks but make frequent mistakes, express frustration, or doubt about their abilities, seek frequent validation and guidance, focus heavily on step-by-step processes, and can describe what to do but struggle to execute smoothly.

Common Mistakes Leaders Make in the Immersion Stage. Leaders often expect perfection too early, don't provide enough real-time feedback, take over when mistakes happen, show frustration with slow progress, and make learners feel inadequate for struggling.

Recognizing When Someone Has Fully Entered the Immersion Stage. Learners have fully entered the Immersion Stage when they recognize gaps in their knowledge, express some doubt or frustration, require close supervision, and make predictable mistakes.

As the Immersion Stage progresses, team members approach a critical juncture in their development journey. This is where many people begin to slide into what we call the Pit of Despair—a crucial transition point between the Immersion Stage and the Empowerment Stage that determines whether development will continue or stall.

Your job is to help learners avoid it.

The Pit of Despair: Where Confidence Collapses

The Pit of Despair is the most difficult—and most defining—part of the development journey. It's the moment when learners hit a wall. What once felt exciting now feels overwhelming. The gap between where they are and where they want to be becomes painfully clear.

Despair typically happens at the end of the Immersion Stage or early in Empowerment if they move backward. They've seen the task, tried it, and realized how far they still have to go. And they start to question everything: "Am I cut out for this?" "Why can't I get it right?" "What if I'm not good enough?"

Here is how employees tend to act when they get close to the Pit of Despair:

- Hesitation and second-guessing
- A drop in initiative
- Increased mistakes and frustration
- Emotional withdrawal or avoidance of new challenges

Why Helping Employees Matters. If leaders don't recognize this moment, team members can get stuck here indefinitely. Growth stalls. Confidence erodes. Potential gets buried. And this will slow everyone down.

Here is how different voices experience the Pit:

- **Nurturers** often withdraw to avoid disappointing others.
- **Creatives** might get lost in conceptual thinking rather than practical application.

- **Guardians** might retreat into procedural concerns and avoid creative risks.
- **Connectors** overrely on relationships instead of developing technical skill.
- **Pioneers** may mask insecurity with overconfidence or rush to other initiatives.

If you are the leader, it is important for you to jump in like this:

- **Name It.** Let learners know this struggle is normal. Say "Most people hit this point—it means you're learning."
- **Increase Support.** This is the time to be present. Offer structure, encouragement, and coaching.
- **Calibrate the Challenge.** Don't rescue learners from struggle, but don't abandon them either. Stay close enough to help, far enough to let them grow.
- **Highlight Progress.** Show them how far they've come. Remind them that growth isn't linear; it happens in fits and starts.

What Not to Do. Don't ignore the signs, don't assume silence means confidence, and don't push too hard without giving feedback loops.

The Goal. Help learners push through this wall; if you guide them well here, they'll build resilience, confidence, and trust—in themselves and in you.

Signs They're Moving Through the Pit. They're moving through the Pit of Despair when they begin to seek solutions rather than dwelling on problems, their questions become more specific and technical, they show willingness to try again after setbacks, and they demonstrate improved skill despite continued struggle.

Successfully navigating through the Pit of Despair is what enables a person to truly enter the Empowerment Stage, where real ownership begins to take shape.

The Empowerment Stage—Conscious Competence—
"You Do, I Help"

When leaders effectively guide team members through the Pit of Despair, something powerful happens: People begin to trust themselves. They gain both competence and confidence—and that's the gateway into the Empowerment Stage.

At this point, learners can perform the task with growing proficiency, but it still takes focus and effort. They're capable but not yet fluent. Mistakes may still happen, but they're learning to correct them on their own.

To help employees in the Empowerment Stage, leaders must:

- Step back to create space for ownership.
- Offer coaching and support without taking over.
- Intervene only when there's real risk of harm or failure.
- Set the stage for success with structure, clarity, and confidence-building feedback.

For example, a salesperson now runs the entire client meeting—from setting the agenda to closing the conversation—while the leader observes quietly, stepping in briefly only if a key point is missed or the meeting veers off-track, then quickly handing control back.

Indicators of Employees in the Empowerment Stage. They complete tasks independently but with deliberate focus, self-correct mistakes before you point them out, seek feedback for improvement rather than validation, can explain their reasoning for decisions, and need only occasional guidance on complex situations.

Common Mistakes Leaders Make at the Empowerment Stage. Leaders often continue to micromanage despite growing competence, don't provide enough critical feedback, fail to celebrate small victories and progress, expect instant mastery without practice, and don't adjust support based on individual needs.

Recognizing When Learners Are Ready for the Multiplication Stage. Learners are ready for the Multiplication Stage when they consistently accomplish tasks with minimal support, troubleshoot problems before bringing them to you, express confidence in their abilities, begin to innovate beyond the standard process, and ask for feedback to refine rather than for direction.

As the Empowerment Stage advances, team members develop increasing competence and confidence in their role. However, before they fully reach the Multiplication Stage, many encounter another critical transition point in their development journey—what we call the Green Room.

The Green Room: Where Growth Gets Comfortable

The Green Room is the most deceptive stage in the development journey. It's the space between Empowerment and true Multiplication—a resting spot that can easily become a trap.

Just like a celebrity waits in the Green Room before going on stage, team members who've become competent and confident can linger here too long. They've mastered the role. They feel trusted. They're no longer in survival mode. But instead of stepping into Multiplication—developing others—they start to enjoy the attention. They like being the favorite. They start to feel a little. . .too secure.

They've stopped pushing forward and started settling in.

Sometimes leaders unintentionally contribute to this problem. The leader is comfortable with this person and trusts them. And instead of calling them up to multiply others, the leader keeps giving them more responsibility—without raising the bar of ownership.

Here is what an employee who is in the Green Room looks like:

- Consistent execution but little initiative to develop others
- Subtle entitlement or overconfidence ("I've earned my spot")
- Resistance to letting go of control or sharing knowledge
- A reluctance to invest in others—especially if it means changing dynamics

The Green Room feels good—for a while. But if people stay there too long, they stall their own growth and stunt the growth of others.

Multiplication doesn't happen. Team capacity flattens. And the leader ends up with strong performers who are no longer growing and not helping others grow either.

Here is how different voices experience the Green Room:

- **Nurturers** may settle into being the go-to helper, avoiding the discomfort of challenging others.
- **Creatives** might stay in the idea zone, hesitant to release their work or mentor practically.
- **Guardians** often get stuck in ownership, reluctant to trust others with their systems.
- **Connectors** enjoy the influence but may avoid the tough relational conversations required to lead others.
- **Pioneers** can grow proud of their success and resist the slower process of bringing others along.

These are the leader's roles in helping people move on from the Green Room:

- **Name It.** Help see where they are. Say "You've earned trust—but now it's time to give it away. Are you ready to multiply?"
- **Raise the Vision.** Recast the goal: not just to be great at your job but to make others great at theirs.
- **Create Stretch Assignments.** Assign mentoring or development tasks that require them to invest in others.
- **Shift the Metrics.** Begin evaluating them not just on what they deliver but on who they're developing.

As a leader, don't take the next actions if you want to help your employees:

- Don't keep piling on responsibilities without changing the expectations.
- Don't reward competence without challenging comfort.

- Don't confuse loyalty with growth; being dependable isn't the same as multiplying.

Help people make the decision to leave the Green Room. The door is open—but they have to choose to walk through it. Your job is to challenge them with belief, not pressure. If they rise to the challenge, they become more than a strong team member: They become a multiplying leader.

Here are the signs that an employee is moving out of the Green Room:

- They initiate development conversations with peers or juniors.
- They begin delegating with intentionality—not just tasking but teaching.
- They ask for guidance on how to grow others, not just themselves.
- They begin to take ownership of culture, not just execution.

Successfully moving beyond the comfort of the Green Room is essential for entering the final stage of development. This transition represents the shift from personal mastery to the multiplication of that mastery in others.

The Multiplication Stage—*Unconscious Competence*— "*You Do, I Watch*"

When leaders effectively challenge team members to move beyond the Green Room, they step into the Multiplication Stage. This is the goal of development: when people no longer need your direction to perform at a high level. They've internalized the skills, can execute with consistency, and begin to think like a leader—anticipating problems, solving them independently, and helping others grow.

They've moved from doing the work to owning it. And now they're ready to pass it on.

When an employee moves to the Multiplication Stage, tasks are completed smoothly without prompting, team members proactively identify and solve problems, they begin training others using the same development process they received, and you've become more of a mentor than a manager.

When this happens, a leader must fully delegate responsibility and trust them to lead, provide occasional feedback but stay out of the day to day, and encourage them to develop others—this is where multiplication begins.

Here is a real-world example. The salesperson now not only leads client meetings independently but has become a go-to mentor for new hires, having internalized the process so well that it feels natural; you check in, but your involvement is minimal, as you've built a leader who builds other leaders.

A successful employee in the Multiplication Stage will perform tasks fluidly with minimal conscious effort, anticipate problems before they arise, adapt processes to improve efficiency, can teach others effectively, and handle complex situations with ease.

If leader continue to check in too frequently, fail to recognize and leverage their expertise, don't create opportunities for the employee to develop others, and neglect to acknowledge the employee's progression to leadership, then they complicate the Development Square and cause many issues.

Being intentional here is what separates effective managers from transformative leaders. You didn't just train someone to do the job; you built someone who can scale your impact.

This is the Development Square. Our goal is to not only help you understand how development works but to customize your leadership by giving you the tools to understand the personality of the person you are leading, which provides insights that are far greater than generic leadership skills.

We want you to become people whisperers so that you can create high-performing cultures that bring true opportunities to lead and work in freedom.

Table 5.1 **Summary of the Leadership Development Journey**

Stage	Dynamic	Leader's Role	Team Member's State
Foundation Stage	"I do, you watch"	Demonstrate, explain, model	Unconscious Incompetence
Immersion Stage	"I do, you help"	Guide, teach, provide feedback	Conscious Incompetence
Empowerment Stage	"You do, I help"	Coach, support, encourage	Building Conscious Competence
Multiplication Stage	"You do, I watch"	Observe, affirm, release	Moving toward Unconscious Competence

Remember: People can be in different stages for different skills. Someone might be in Stage 4 for technical skills but Stage 1 for people management.

The Leadership Development Journey Summarized

The above table summarizes the leadership development journey.

The Psychology Behind Development

Abraham Maslow, known for his Hierarchy of Needs, taught that human motivation follows a progression—people must have their basic needs met before they can grow into higher levels of performance and fulfillment. That same principle applies directly to leadership development.

If team members don't feel secure, don't have clear direction, or lack the support to succeed, they won't progress. Instead, they'll become frustrated, disengaged, or stuck in place.

No one becomes a high-performing leader overnight. People need structure, encouragement, and a clear pathway forward.

This development concept was introduced by Noel Burch, who worked at Gordon Training International, who understood that growth is incremental, that people need frameworks that simplify complexity, and that both leaders and learners benefit from having a shared language to describe their development journey. They built on Maslow's internally focused theory of motivation by adding practical, external tools for behavioral development.

At GiANT Worldwide, we've expanded that model by adding the Pit of Despair and the Green Room as well as stages surrounding the square, making it easier to identify where someone is in their development—and what they need from you next. Even more, we have added the hyper-personalization tool of the 5 Voices to make leader development highly contextual and potent.

Visualizing Voice-Driven Leadership

This Voice-Driven Leader graphic (Figure 5.2) shows how the 5 Voices added to the Development Square creates a hyper-personalized development roadmap.

Imagine a leader who is a Pioneer—results-driven, fast-paced, and future-focused. That leader is coaching five different team members, each with a different Voice. Each of those team members is also at a different point in the Development Square—from Foundation to Empowerment.

The challenge of modern leadership is that:

- One-size-fits-all doesn't work.
- Each person needs something different based on their Voice and their current stage of competence.
- The Pioneer leader must slow down to lead each individual well, even when slower is not their natural pace.
- A leader is typically leading multiple people with different voices at different stages at the same time.

Voice-Driven leadership is the real work of leadership. And it's what separates managers who delegate from leaders who develop.

VOICE-DRIVEN LEADER

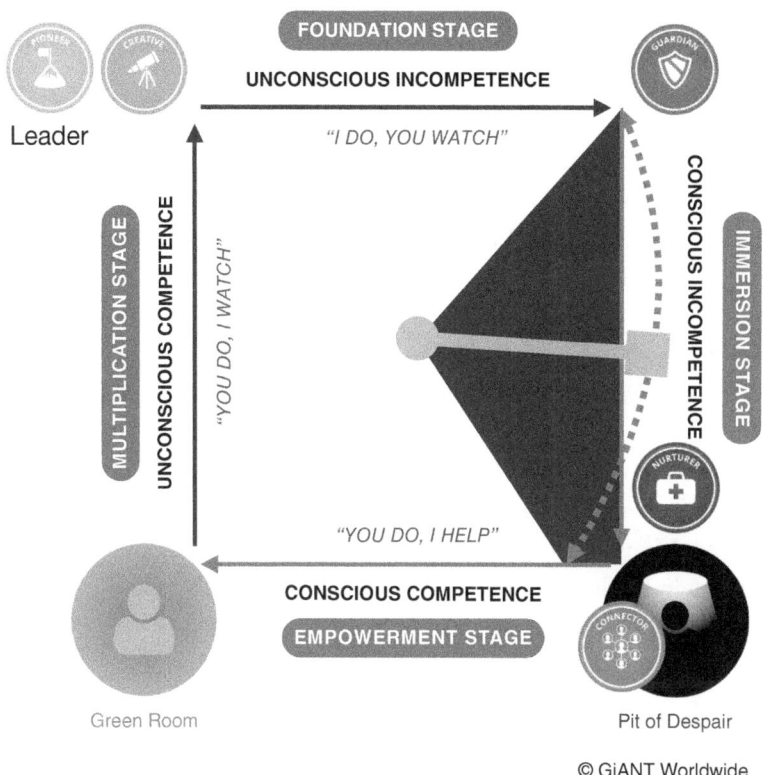

Source Credit: A. Maslow, Gordon Training International

Figure 5.2   Voice-Driven Leader Map

What Developing Others Looks Like in Real Life

Kim was still finding her footing at InfoSystems when Jason, the new chief financial officer, arrived. InfoSystems—a leading cybersecurity firm based in Chattanooga, Tennessee—was thriving, but Kim wasn't in her sweet spot. She wasn't a tech expert. Her role focused on administration and internal operations, and while she managed entry-level accounting tasks, she seemed underutilized, disconnected, and lacking clear direction.

As Jason stepped into his new role, he prioritized building trust with the team. One of the first tools he introduced was the 5 Voices framework, something he'd learned from his certified 5 Voices guide, Dwayne Morris. Jason had seen firsthand how this tool could unlock potential by increasing self-awareness, improving communication, and helping people find their leadership lane.

It didn't take long for Jason to see that Kim had leadership potential. But her Nurturer Voice, while caring and dependable, made her hesitant to step into more responsibility—especially in the more analytical side of accounting. She lacked confidence and was stuck in unconscious incompetence—she didn't even realize what she didn't know.

Jason saw this as an opportunity for growth. Through consistent one-on-one meetings, he used the Developing Others tool shown in the Development Square (Figure 5.1) to help Kim understand her natural leadership tendencies and build confidence in areas she avoided. He wasn't trying to fix her; he was equipping her. His first goal? Help her lead herself well so she could lead others in the future.

One key area of development was financial analysis. Jason began walking Kim through spreadsheets step by step, explaining how the numbers connected to broader business decisions. At first, she just observed. But over time, he started sending her sheets to analyze on her own. Slowly Kim's confidence grew. She wasn't just learning the concepts—she was starting to believe she could master them.

Then something unexpected happened.

One afternoon, Kim's mom stopped by the office to drop something off. She chatted briefly with Jason, then pulled him aside and said, "I don't know exactly what you're doing, but my daughter is a completely different person. I can't tell you how much it means to see her confidence grow like this."

That moment stuck with Jason. Later, Kim shared more of her story. Before Jason arrived, the culture had taken a toll on her. Her confidence had been crushed, and she was planning to leave the company. She didn't see a future—until someone gave her a chance to grow.

Jason appreciated the kind words, but he knew this wasn't about him. It was about using the right tools in the right way. He simply followed the Developing Others framework, stayed consistent, and helped Kim grow through strategic coaching and real opportunity.

But the work wasn't done.

Jason knew that growth can stall if people retreat into comfort. He kept challenging Kim, knowing she was approaching the Pit of Despair—the make-or-break moment where leaders either level up or pull back. Kim pushed forward.

Soon a shift happened. Kim no longer needed Jason's approval for every decision. She led meetings, made confident choices, and started mentoring others. What once felt daunting had become second nature. She had moved into unconscious competence—and into leadership.

By investing in Kim, Jason wasn't just helping one person. He was strengthening the organization. Her growth created momentum. As the team expanded, Kim became a key player in onboarding and developing others. What began as a quiet investment turned into a multiplying effect.

This is the goal. We want you to be equipped to develop others—thoroughly, intentionally, and effectively. When you do, you create a positive growth culture that builds leaders.

This isn't just true at work, the same is true at home, with kids.

What Parenting Teaches Us About Leadership Development

One of the most intuitive ways to understand how people grow is through parenting. Developing employees follows a surprisingly similar pattern—just with fewer bedtime stories and more spreadsheets.

Great parenting—and great leadership—requires the same core elements: intentional coaching, not assumption; progressive freedom as skills increase; and a healthy balance of challenge and support.

Let's walk through the Development Square from a parenting perspective.

The Four Stages of Parenting and Leadership Development

Foundation Stage: I Do, You Watch (Ages 0–5). This is the modeling stage. Children (or new employees) watch how things are done. The goal isn't independence; it's exposure. Parents model behavior, routines, and expectations, just like leaders do during onboarding.

Immersion Stage: I Do, You Help (Ages 5–12). Now they want to participate. Kids begin helping in small ways—making their bed, setting the table—still under close supervision. It's about building confidence through guided practice.

Engagement Stage: You Do, I Help (Ages 13–18). Adolescents are taking more ownership, but they still need coaching. They want autonomy, but they don't always have the judgment to go it alone. The same is true for developing employees at the Empowerment Stage. They can execute but still benefit from strategic support and feedback.

Multiplication Stage: You Do, I Watch (Ages 18+). The goal of parenting is to launch your kids well. College, a job, adulthood—they're doing it on their own, and you're in the background. If they still need you to drive every decision, something went wrong earlier. The same applies in leadership: Your people should be able to thrive without your constant oversight.

You wouldn't push a child onto a bike and yell "Good luck!" That's a fast track to injury and tears.

Instead, a wise parent:

- Holds the seat.
- Runs alongside them.
- Offers encouragement.
- Gradually lets go as they build balance and confidence.

It's the same with leadership. Without structure, coaching, and progressive freedom, people flounder. They freeze, fall, or fake it. But with intentional development, they find their balance and move forward with confidence.

You lead people forward not by force but by earning the right to walk beside them.

Remember, each new skill or responsibility requires its own journey through the square.

Now let's dive into the Foundation Stage and explore how to lead people well from the very beginning.

6

The Foundation Stage

"I Do, You Watch"

You wouldn't hand a child the keys to a car and expect them to drive without lessons, so why do so many leaders throw new hires into the deep end and expect them to swim?

The Foundation Stage (see Figure 6.1) is not a formality; it's a defining moment. It sets the tone for how quickly and effectively someone will grow in their role. This stage is where leadership development truly begins.

To lead effectively in this critical onboarding stage, it is important to understand what team members are experiencing.

Understanding the Foundation Stage

From the perspective of new employees, everything is new. New team. New expectations. New systems. They don't know what they don't know yet—and that's okay. But it also means that early confidence is

STAGE ONE: **THE FOUNDATION**

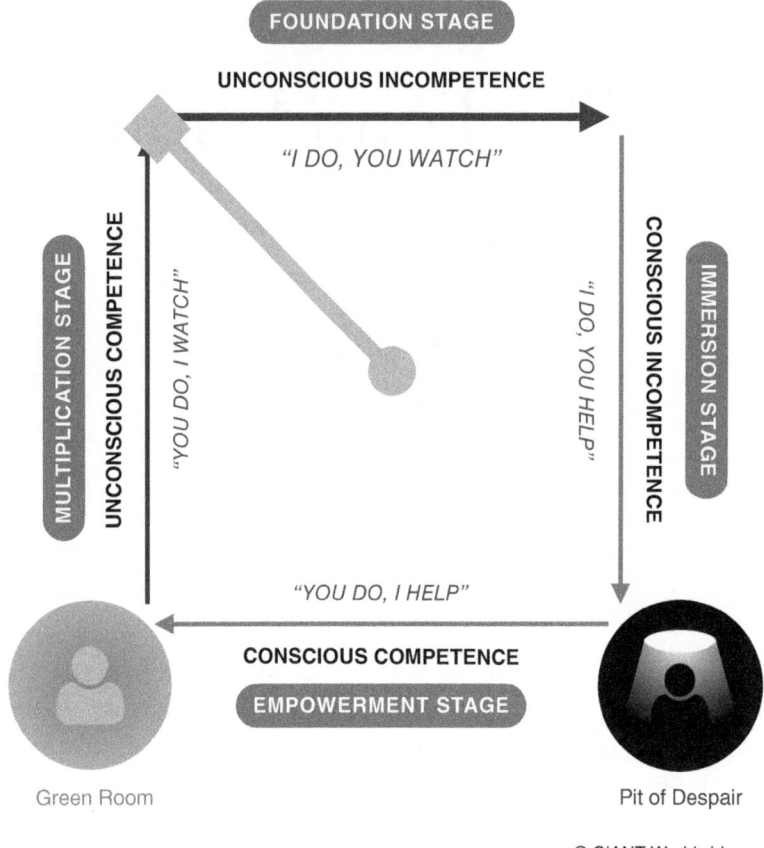

Source Credit: A. Maslow, Gordon Training International

Figure 6.1   The Foundation Stage

often misplaced. Excitement is high, but it's built on assumptions, not understanding.

Their mindset might sound like this:

- "This is exciting!"
- "I've got this."

- "I want to impress my manager."
- "Wait. . .this is more complicated than I expected."
- "I hope I don't mess this up."

At this stage, new employees are in Unconscious Incompetence—they don't yet realize how much they don't know. And if we're not careful, their initial optimism can quickly become anxiety and hesitation.

The leader's job? Provide clarity, structure, and modeling. Not just what to do, but how and why to do it well.

How People Learn Best at This Stage

At the Foundation Stage, team members are in learning mode, not execution mode. They absorb more by watching than doing. The leader's goal is to help them observe with intentionality and begin building the mental framework needed for future success.

Here's how learning sticks best at this stage:

- **Observation.** Let them shadow experienced team members. They're soaking in tone, language, and decision making—far beyond what's written in a handbook.
- **Clear Demonstration.** Show the task step by step. Don't just explain what you're doing; narrate your thought process as you go.
- **Guided Reflection.** Ask questions that spark insight. Try "What did you notice?" or "Why do you think we handled it that way?"
- **Repetition with Purpose.** Revisit key tasks multiple times, each time adding a layer of understanding.

Your job here isn't just to do the work; it's to help team members learn how work is done.

What Can Go Wrong

If a leader assumes enthusiasm equals understanding, this stage can go off course quickly. Rushing through onboarding or assuming people will "figure it out" leads to bad habits formed early that are hard to break, false confidence that crashes when real complexity shows up, and disengagement when clarity and direction are missing.

When people don't feel safe to ask questions, they either pretend they understand or shut down. That's how potential gets lost.

Given these potential pitfalls, how can you create the right environment for growth? Let's look at what team members need in this stage.

What They Need from You as a Leader

This is your chance to set the tone. The best leaders at the Foundation Stage are intentional, present, and patient. Your team needs you to set expectations clearly with "Here's what success looks like right now"; encourage observation over performance by saying "Just watch for now—we'll talk through it after"; normalize the learning curve with "You're not expected to know this yet. That's why I'm showing you"; and check in proactively by asking "What questions do you have so far?" rather than waiting for them to speak up.

Done well, this stage builds confidence, establishes trust, and accelerates learning later.

When Are They Ready to Move On?

The Foundation Stage isn't about doing; it's about understanding. You'll know someone is ready to move into the Immersion Stage ("I Do, You Help") when they:

People don't grow by jumping into the deep end; they grow when leaders show them how to swim.

- Begin asking thoughtful questions
- Can predict the next step in a process
- Understand not just what's happening but why
- Express readiness to try a small part of the work

Now that we have shared the fundamentals of the Foundation Stage, let's explore how each Voice uniquely experiences it.

Voice-Specific Guidance

In the Foundation Stage, every individual brings their unique strengths, struggles, and learning preferences. Some Voices are eager to dive in while others prefer to observe cautiously. Recognizing these differences helps leaders provide the right balance of guidance, challenge, and encouragement.

The Nurturer (Present-Oriented, People-Focused)

Mindset. "I want to get this right because people are counting on me."

The Experience. Nurturers enter the Foundation Stage with a strong desire to contribute, but they tend to be cautious, fearing that mistakes will let others down. They watch closely, trying to absorb every detail before acting. While they may hesitate to ask questions, they are deeply committed to learning and doing things correctly. If they feel safe, they will become eager participants; if they feel overwhelmed or criticized, they may retreat.

Learning Strengths of a Nurturer:

+ Highly observant—notice subtle cues and unspoken expectations.
+ Relationally driven—want to make a positive impact on the team
+ Dependable—committed to learning the right way to do things

Common Struggles of a Nurturer:

− Hesitate to ask questions for fear of burdening others
− Internalize mistakes as personal failures rather than learning experiences
− May struggle with direct or impersonal feedback, needing more encouragement

Leader's Tip. Reassure them that mistakes are a natural part of learning, provide encouragement before offering constructive feedback, use team-oriented language like "When you learn this, the whole team benefits," and create a safe space for asking questions by checking in proactively.

The Creative (Future-Oriented, Vision-Focused)

Mindset. "How does this fit into the bigger picture?"

The Experience. Creatives enter the Foundation Stage with excitement about possibilities but skepticism about structure. They are deep thinkers who want to understand the "why" behind a task before fully engaging in the "how." If they can't connect the task to a bigger purpose, they may disengage or challenge the process. While highly imaginative, they can overcomplicate simple tasks or become frustrated if they don't feel their perspective is valued.

Learning Strengths of a Creative:

+ Conceptual thinkers—quickly recognize patterns and deeper meaning
+ Curious and imaginative—love exploring new ways to improve processes
+ See long-term impact—connect the present task to future outcomes

Common Struggles of a Creative:

- Overthink simple steps, making things more complex than necessary
- Get frustrated by too many details without understanding the purpose
- May challenge the process too early, believing they see a better way

Leader's Tip. Connect tasks to the bigger vision by saying "This step is crucial because it sets the foundation for. . ."; encourage curiosity but anchor it in execution; celebrate insights while helping them focus on fundamentals first; and provide room for questions but keep them progressing through the task.

The Guardian (Present-Oriented, Process-Focused)

Mindset. "Just show me the right way to do it."

The Experience. Guardians approach the Foundation Stage with practical curiosity, eager to learn but frustrated by ambiguity. They thrive in structured environments and want clear, step-by-step instructions. If expectations are inconsistent or training is disorganized, they may become skeptical or resistant. They prefer a methodical approach and can struggle when thrown into unstructured learning situations.

Learning Strengths of a Guardian:

+ Detail-oriented—retain information best when it's well structured
+ Respect established best practices and procedures
+ Dependable—consistent and reliable in following through

Common Struggles of a Guardian

− Resist unstructured or trial-and-error learning
− Feel stressed when mistakes aren't clearly diagnosed and addressed
− Get frustrated when leaders deviate from established processes

Leader's Tip. Provide step-by-step instructions with clear rationale, use logical explanations to reinforce understanding, acknowledge their precision and invite them to suggest process improvements, and keep expectations structured as consistency builds their confidence.

The Connector (Future-Oriented, People-Focused)

Mindset. "Who will this help, and how can we make this fun?"

The Experience. Connectors enter the Foundation Stage full of enthusiasm and energy. They thrive in interactive, social learning environments but may lose interest if the learning process feels repetitive or disconnected from relationships. If training is too rigid or lacks personal connection, they may disengage, seeking out side conversations instead of focusing on the task.

Learning Strengths of a Connector:
+ Highly engaged in collaborative and interactive settings
+ Learn best through storytelling, discussion, and real-world applications
+ Quickly reinforce learning by sharing insights with others

Common Struggles of a Connector:
− Lose focus during highly detailed, monotonous instruction
− Get impatient with repetitive tasks or slow processes
− May struggle with consistency if learning lacks relational elements

Leader's Tip. Make learning interactive through discussions, storytelling, and role-playing, connect the task to who it impacts by saying "This will help us build better client relationships," and encourage them to teach others quickly to reinforce their learning.

The Pioneer (Future-Oriented, Results-Focused)

Mindset. "How quickly can I get good at this?"

The Experience. Pioneers enter the Foundation Stage with confidence and high expectations. They assume they will pick up tasks quickly and may underestimate the complexity of the process. If the learning feels slow or overly detailed, they become impatient and may cut corners. They are naturally competitive and thrive when the process is framed as a challenge.

Learning Strengths of a Pioneer:
+ Confident and goal-driven—want to master tasks quickly
+ Thrive when the task is framed as a challenge to overcome
+ Willing to take risks and learn through trial and error

Common Struggles of a Pioneer:
- Impatient with step-by-step instruction; prefer action
- Resistant to feedback if they feel it slows them down
- May skip foundational steps in eagerness to reach mastery

Leader's Tip. Frame the learning process as a strategic challenge by saying "Mastering this will help you lead bigger projects," allow controlled risk taking while ensuring core steps are mastered, use metrics and measurable goals to maintain engagement, and keep feedback direct and tied to outcomes while avoiding micromanaging.

Recognizing the Needs of Each Voice

No two people experience the Foundation Stage the same way. Some want structure. Others want freedom. Some need encouragement. Others need a challenge. The best leaders don't treat everyone the same; they adapt their approach to fit each person's Voice.

We want you to understand the real needs of each Voice so they can thrive in the Foundation Stage.

- **Nurturers** need reassurance that mistakes are normal, and growth takes time. They thrive in a safe, supportive environment.
- **Creatives** need to see how the task connects to the bigger picture. When they understand the "why," they'll engage with the "how."
- **Guardians** need structure. Clear expectations and step-by-step instruction give them the confidence to move forward.
- **Connectors** need interaction. They learn best through people, stories, and collaboration—especially when they see they can make an impact on people.
- **Pioneers** need to be challenged. Fast-paced, results-driven environments energize them—but they also need reminders to master the basics first.

Table 6.1   Cheat Sheet: How Each Voice Learns in the Foundation Stage

Voice	Learning Preference	Primary Frustration	Best Leadership Approach
Nurturer	Relational, patient instruction	Harsh feedback or feeling like a burden	Build trust with encouragement and clarity
Creative	Vision-first, concept-based learning	Tasks without a clear "why"	Connect learning to the bigger picture
Guardian	Structure and step-by-step processes	Ambiguity or process inconsistency	Provide clear documentation and logic
Connector	Interactive, social learning	Boring, isolated training	Make learning interactive and purpose-driven
Pioneer	Action-oriented, challenge-based learning	Slow, repetitive processes	Create challenges that lead to mastery

Great leaders don't treat everyone the same. They lead each person in the way they learn best.

When leaders recognize and respond to these differences, the Foundation Stage becomes more than an introduction—it becomes a launchpad for long-term growth.

To help you quickly apply these insights with your team, the next cheat sheet (Table 6.1) provides a practical reference guide.

Strengths and Challenges for Leaders Leading in the Foundation Stage

The 5 Leadership Voices shape how we develop others. Each Voice excels at certain elements but also has areas of growth that, if not

Table 6.2 Leaders' Strengths and Challenges in the Foundation Stage

Voice	Natural Strengths	Common Mistakes
Nurturer	Encouraging, patient, makes people feel safe	Avoids direct feedback, assumes people will ask for help
Creative	Inspires learning, connects tasks to a bigger vision	Overcomplicates things, introduces too many new ideas at once
Guardian	Provides clear structure, ensures consistency	Can be overly rigid, may overwhelm people with too much detail
Connector	Creates excitement, keeps engagement high	Moves too quickly, assumes people "get it" without checking
Pioneer	Pushes people toward mastery, expects high performance	Too fast-paced, assumes learning happens through trial and error

addressed, can hinder development. The above table shows the strengths and typical mistakes of leaders based on their own foundational voice.

When leaders recognize their natural tendencies, they can adjust their coaching style to accelerate learning for those they lead.

Unfortunately, we have found that the Foundation Stage is often overlooked or rushed in practice. Let's examine why this happens and the consequences.

Why Most Leaders Skip the Foundation Stage

Let's be honest: Most leaders want independent, capable team members as quickly as possible. But in the rush to get results, they often skip the most critical stage of development.

Leaders often rationalize not developing people in this stage with statements like "I hired smart people. They'll figure it out," "They've seen me do it once. I don't need to explain it," or "If they have questions, they'll ask."

But the fundamental problem is that watching isn't the same as understanding.

When leaders skip the Foundation Stage, three things inevitably happen:

1. **Confusion Sets in.** Without clear modeling and expectations, new team members don't know what "good" looks like. So they guess—or wait for direction.
2. **Mistakes Multiply.** Bad habits form early. Without real-time feedback or clear guidance, small errors compound into bigger ones.
3. **Frustration Builds.** Both the leader and the team member feel stuck. The leader thinks, "Why can't they just get it?" and the team member thinks, "Why didn't anyone teach me this?"

The irony is that in trying to go fast, leaders who skip the Foundation Stage actually slow everything down.

The reality is that people don't fail because they're incapable; they fail when leaders assume they'll figure it out on their own.

Confusion, rework, and disengagement cost far more time than thoughtful onboarding ever would. Great leaders know: If you want people to move fast later, you have to slow down to speed up.

Two Leaders, Two Outcomes

Let's compare two leaders with the same goal—developing a new team member.

Sarah slows down to speed up. She walks her new hire through each step of the role. She explains not just what to do but why it matters. She creates a safe space for questions and makes it clear: You're not expected to be perfect—just willing to learn.

Three months later? That team member is solving problems, asking better questions, and stepping into ownership. They're confident— and ready for the next stage of development.

Mark assumes they'll figure it out. He points to a few resources, gives the team member a quick overview, and moves on to the next thing. When mistakes happen, he jumps in to fix them rather than teaching in the moment.

Three months later? His team members are unsure, hesitant, and dependent. They're still waiting for direction and afraid to take initiative.

Who's at fault? Mark might say "I hired the wrong person." But the truth is, he skipped the Foundation Stage. The difference between Sarah and Mark wasn't talent; it was intention.

Let's now explore how you can intentionally create the conditions for growth in your own team.

Setting the Stage for Growth

The Foundation Stage isn't about perfection. It's about giving people the clarity and confidence they need to grow.

Every new beginning—whether it's a new hire, a promotion, or a shift in responsibilities—brings both excitement and uncertainty. In the early days in a new role, people are forming their first impressions of what success looks like. That's why the foundation stage is so important.

The Foundation Stage, also known as "I Do, You Watch," is where learning truly begins. And how you lead during this stage determines how quickly—and how well—someone develops.

The mistake most leaders make? They skip this stage. They assume talented people will figure things out and hope initiative will cover gaps in instruction. But hope isn't a development strategy. If you want confident, capable team members, you must slow down and teach them the right way from the start.

Here is what the Foundation Stage looks like:

- "I Do, You Watch." You demonstrate while they observe.
- You explain not just what to do, but why it matters.
- You invite questions and help them connect the dots.
- You establish expectations and create a safe space for learning.

When done well, the Foundation Stage will help:

- People feel safe.
- Learning habits strengthen.
- Confidence begin.
- Create a path toward hands-on engagement appears.

When the Foundation stage is skipped, people will become:

- Confused about expectations.
- Disengaged, leading to self-doubt.
- Dependent on the leader.
- Careless, leading to mistakes.

The choice is yours: Rush ahead and deal with setbacks—or slow down and set the stage for sustainable growth.

Too many leaders think onboarding is someone else's job—or that smart people will just "figure it out." But great leaders treat onboarding as the first step in leadership development.

Onboarding isn't orientation; it's the start of someone's leadership journey.

It's where culture is transferred. It's where expectations are clarified. It's where future performance begins.

Practical Tips for Effective Onboarding

The Foundation Stage is where confidence, clarity, and competence begin. A structured onboarding process turns new hires into productive team members faster—and with fewer setbacks.

Table 6.3 Tips for Effective Onboarding

Tip	What It Looks Like
Assign a learning guide	Pair the new team member with an experienced colleague who models excellence and explains as they work.
Introduce the Development Square	Walk new team members through the stages of development so they know where they are and what's coming next.
Normalize the Pit of Despair	Explain that struggle is part of the process: "It's normal to feel unsure before you get confident."
Provide real-time feedback	Give frequent, gentle course corrections before bad habits set in. Stay encouraging while being clear.
Celebrate small wins	Reinforce momentum: "You handled that client email perfectly—great attention to tone and timing."

The above table provides tips for leaders to make onboarding practical and powerful.

Strong starts build strong contributors.

Your job is to create an environment where new team members learn quickly, feel safe, and build the right habits early. Don't outsource onboarding; own it.

Leader's Challenge: Build the Right Foundation

If you want a high-performing team, you must first become a high-intentional leader. That starts with how you onboard and train in the Foundation Stage.

This week, choose one team member—especially someone new, recently promoted, or struggling in a current role—and take these five steps:

1. Identify a critical task they need to learn.
2. Demonstrate it slowly and clearly, narrating your thought process as you go.

3. Ask reflective questions: "What stood out to you? What questions do you have?"
4. Give them time to observe, without pressure to jump in too fast.
5. Set clear expectations for what learning looks like in this stage: "Right now, your job is to watch and learn. We'll move to practice soon."

Then ask yourself: Am I developing this person intentionally—or hoping they figure it out?

In the next chapter, we explore how to lead effectively during the Immersion Stage, where your role shifts from demonstrator to coach as team members begin their hands-on journey.

7

The Immersion Stage

"I Do, You Help"

The Immersion Stage, shown in Figure 7.1, is a pivotal point in leadership development. It's the moment when individuals begin to step out of observation and into participation. It's where confidence is fragile, mistakes are frequent, and leaders are tested just as much as their teams.

I (Jeremie) remember the first time I tried to let go. I had a bright, capable team member—eager, smart, and ready to contribute. I handed her part of a critical project and made two key mistakes. First, I didn't give her enough guidance. I assumed she'd figure it out. She didn't. Then, when she struggled, I jumped in and took over—robbing her of the chance to learn and build confidence. The result? She pulled back, I stayed overworked, and she hesitated to step up again.

That's when I realized: The Immersion Stage isn't just about what the team member is learning; it's also about what the leader is learning.

STAGE TWO: **IMMERSION**

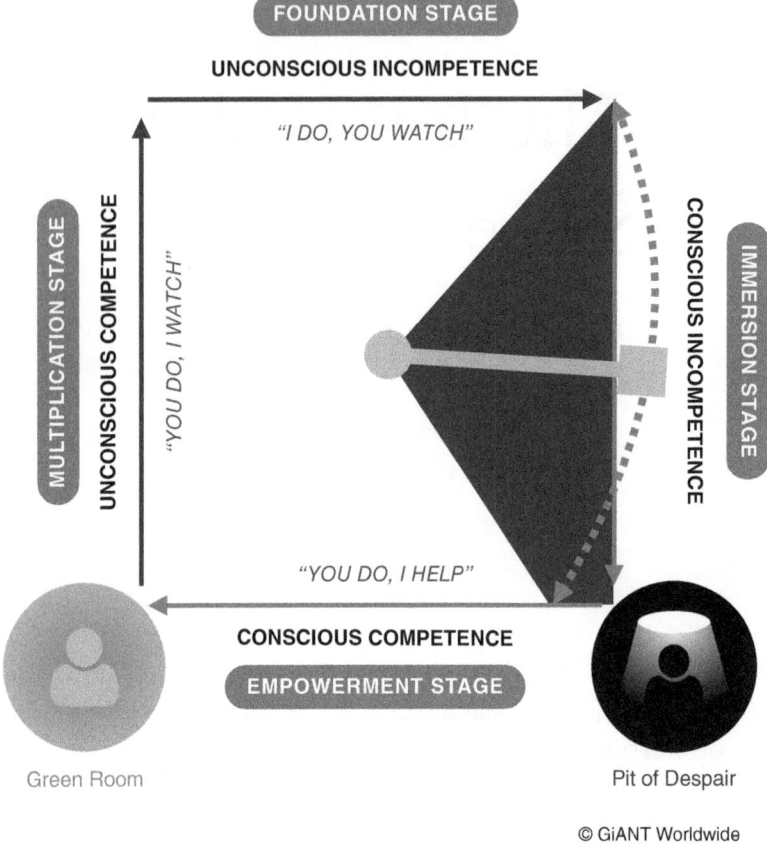

Green Room　　　　　　　　　　　　　　　Pit of Despair

© GiANT Worldwide

Source Credit: A. Maslow, Gordon Training International

Figure 7.1　The Immersion Stage: Creating a Space for Safe Development

The Critical Transition from Watching to Doing

If the Foundation Stage is about modeling great execution, the Immersion Stage is where you invite your team into the process. It's the shift from observation to participation—where team members move from watching you to working alongside you.

The key is this: They're still helping, but they're not yet leading. This stage follows the "I Do, You Help" pattern. Here's what it looks like in action:

- The leader remains the primary executor but involves the team in small, meaningful parts of the task.
- The team member learns by doing, with real-time guidance and correction.
- The environment is structured and safe for learning—mistakes are expected and supported.

At this point, both parties feel the tension. The team member wants to grow but doesn't feel fully ready. The leader wants to develop others but worries about letting go. The balance between control and empowerment is delicate—and often determines whether someone will step up or step back.

This stage is where leadership transforms from directing to coaching. The focus shifts from merely completing tasks to developing your team's capabilities while accomplishing meaningful work together.

Like a Sherpa guiding climbers up Mount Everest, skilled team leaders in the Immersion Stage don't just point toward the summit; they climb alongside their team, providing exactly the right support at each challenging step. They know when to offer a steady hand and when to let team members test their footing on difficult terrain. This calibrated approach helps people reach new heights they couldn't achieve alone.

The Immersion Stage is about striking that delicate balance—creating enough structure to prevent failure while allowing enough freedom to foster growth. Your team members are no longer just observers; they're active participants in their own development journey. And you, as their leader, are both their guide and their safety net.

> *Growth happens when leaders show the way.*

Leading Like a 100X Leader

In *The 100X Leader*, we introduced the idea that the Sherpa on Mount Everest represents what great leaders actually do—they are guides who climb the mountain with their team, not ahead of them or from a distance.[1] Sherpas are elite leaders. Their job isn't just to reach the summit—it's to help others get there safely and successfully.

That's what effective leadership looks like in the Immersion Stage.

Sherpa-style leaders don't just bark orders or hand off tasks. They:

- Climb ahead to clear the path and identify the safest route.
- Support their climbers with exactly what they need for the next step.
- Challenge and encourage along the way, never letting people settle.

That's your job now.

In this stage, your team is learning by doing, but they still need guardrails. You're there to:

- Model what great execution looks like.
- Coach as they participate alongside you.
- Step in when they're stuck—but not before they've had the chance to try.

Leadership in the Immersion Stage is about guiding, not carrying.

Get too hands-off, and team members will feel abandoned. Get too hands-on, and they'll become dependent. The key is calibrating support and challenge to match their growth.

---

[1] Kubicek, J. and Cockram, S. (2019). *The 100X Leader: How to Become Someone Worth Following*. Wiley.

Just like a Sherpa, you don't carry your team; you equip them to climb.

Why Some Leaders Struggle with This Stage

Stepping into the Immersion Stage requires leaders to recalibrate their instincts. As a leader, you must resist the temptation to rescue team members at every stumble while ensuring they don't feel abandoned when they need guidance.

The three most common challenges leaders face during this stage are the overcontrol problem, the thrown-in-the-deep-end problem, and the fear of letting people struggle.

The Overcontrol Problem

Some leaders, especially Guardians and Pioneers, have difficulty letting go. They believe that "it's faster if I just do it myself."

Take Laura, a Guardian leader in finance. She was known for her precision and high standards. When she hired a new financial analyst, she micromanaged every task. If he made a mistake, she fixed it herself rather than helping him learn. Over time, the analyst stopped taking initiative, relying on Laura's corrections.

Laura's attempt to maintain high-quality work backfired. She remained overburdened, and her team stopped growing.

The Thrown-in-the-Deep-End Problem

Other leaders, especially Pioneers and Connectors, believe that the best way to learn is to have people "just jump in."

Ryan, a Pioneer leading a startup, assumed his junior engineer would "figure it out" during a client call. But without preparation, the engineer fumbled through the conversation, frustrating the client and damaging the relationship.

Ryan thought he was encouraging independence. In reality, he was setting his team up to fail.

The Fear of Letting People Struggle

Some leaders hesitate to let their team members struggle. Their desire to protect others from discomfort robs team members of valuable growth opportunities.

If you always shield your team from struggle, you also block their path to learning.

Jessica, a Nurturer in healthcare, assigned a junior nurse to lead a staff meeting but, at the last minute, stepped in to "help." The nurse lost a crucial opportunity to practice and remained anxious about public speaking.

Where Leaders Struggle in the Immersion Stage

In the next table, we show where leaders struggle in the Immersion Stage, based on the leader's Voice.

The Challenge of Conscious Incompetence

Conscious Incompetence is one of the most difficult phases in the development journey. It's the moment when reality hits—when people realize just how much they don't yet know. The early enthusiasm wears off, and the learning curve starts to feel steep.

This phase is where frustration kicks in and confidence begins to wobble. For many people, it's their first real taste of meaningful struggle. They've moved from watching to doing, but now the mistakes feel more personal, and the gap between "wanting to get it right" and "actually doing it right" feels wide.

This stage is critical for two reasons:

1. It's a tipping point. People will either push through the discomfort or start to disengage.
2. It reveals your leadership. How you respond in this moment determines whether people grow or stall.

Table 7.1 Where Leaders Struggle in the Immersion Stage

Leader Type	Common Struggle	What Happens	Leadership Insight
Nurturer	Avoids letting others struggle	Steps in too quickly Team misses growth moments	Protecting too much stunts confidence and resilience
Creative	Assumes others can "see the vision"	Fails to provide clear steps Others get lost in ambiguity	Big ideas need practical structure to turn into progress
Guardian	Overcontrolling; perfectionistic	Fixes mistakes instead of coaching Team loses initiative	Micromanagement maintains quality but kills development
Connector	Overestimates readiness	Assumes enthusiasm equals capability Team feels overwhelmed	Energy doesn't equal execution Guide before handing off
Pioneer	Throws people in too soon	Delegates before people are ready Performance and confidence suffer	Bold moves require preparation and support

As a leader, your job is to normalize the discomfort without minimizing it. Struggle isn't a sign of failure; it's a necessary part of the learning process. But if your team members feel unsupported or misunderstood in this phase, they'll lose belief in themselves.

That's where understanding each person's Voice becomes crucial. All Voices react differently when they hit Conscious Incompetence. Some retreat. Some power through. Some get stuck in their heads. And your coaching must adjust accordingly.

The next section walks through how each of the 5 Voices responds in this phase—and what they need most from you as their leader.

How Each Voice Handles Conscious Incompetence

The next Voice-by-Voice breakdown shows how each person responds during the Immersion Stage—along with what they need from you to stay out of the Pit of Despair.

Each Voice needs a different blend of support and challenge. The more you can tailor your coaching to team members' natural wiring, the faster they'll move from the Immersion Stage (Conscious Incompetence) to the Empowerment Stage (Conscious Competence).

Why This Stage Matters So Much

The Immersion Stage is a turning point in leadership development.

This is where confidence is tested, growth begins, and your influence as a leader either expands or stalls. You are no longer just executing; you're building future leaders through intentional, hands-on guidance.

If the Foundation Stage is about showing what good looks like, the Immersion Stage is where your people begin to try it for themselves—with you by their side.

And that's what makes this stage so critical. It's where:

- **Belief is Built or Broken.** A team member's confidence will either take root—or collapse—based on how you lead during their first real attempts.

Table 7.2 How Voices Handle Conscious Incompetence

Voice	Mindset	What Triggers the Pit	What They Need from You
Nurturer	"I don't want to let anyone down."	Feeling they've disappointed the team or let someone down Overly critical feedback Lack of emotional support	Encouragement Reassurance that learning helps the team A safe space to ask questions
Creative	"Why isn't this working like I imagined?"	Tasks that don't connect to a bigger purpose Feeling dismissed or misunderstood Overly rigid structures	Tie task to vision and purpose Break things into clear steps. Affirm their ideas as they grow
Guardian	"I need to get this right."	Unclear expectations Fast-moving environments Mistakes due to missing details	Provide structure and process Give clear, step-by-step instructions Normalize mistakes as part of learning
Connector	"Why isn't this more fun?"	Boring or repetitive tasks Lack of relational engagement Feeling disconnected from team	Keep process interactive Celebrate small wins Show how work connects to people and outcomes
Pioneer	"Why am I not good at this yet?"	Slow progress Micromanagement Feeling stuck without quick wins	Frame learning as a challenge Set short-term goals Let them own progress and track success

- **Learning Becomes Real.** The Immersion Stage is where abstract ideas are tested through practice. Mistakes will happen, but so will progress—if you stay engaged.
- **Leadership Capacity Begins to Multiply.** The effort you put in here pays off in future stages, as team members learn to take ownership and build toward independence.

> *The Immersion Stage is where development either takes off or breaks down. Your presence makes the difference.*

But none of that happens automatically.

It takes a leader who's willing to walk the tightrope between support and challenge. One who can coach in the moment, resist the urge to take over, and build confidence—even when results are shaky.

Done well, the Immersion Stage lays the foundation for sustainable growth—growth that doesn't rely on you doing all the work but on you developing others to do it well.

What Success Looks Like

When the Immersion Stage is working, you'll begin to see subtle—but powerful—shifts. Your team members aren't fully independent yet, but they're gaining traction. They're still learning, but they're learning faster. And most important, they're starting to believe they can do it.

Here are the key signs that development is moving in the right direction:

- **Initiative Increases.** Team members begin volunteering to help or take on parts of the task without being asked.
- **Mistakes are Made—and Recovered from.** Team members don't fall apart when something goes wrong. Instead, they learn, adapt, and bounce back.

- **Their Questions Improve.** Instead of just asking for instructions, team members begin asking thoughtful questions that show deeper understanding.
- **Ideas Begin to Emerge.** Team members contribute suggestions, offer improvements, and show curiosity about the bigger picture.
- **Your Role Starts to Shift.** You're still leading, but you're doing more coaching than directing.

When these signs appear, you will know that the employee is moving in the right direction.

Leader's Reflection: How Well Are You Leading in the Immersion Stage?

Use the Immersion Stage assessment to evaluate your leadership habits during this critical stage of development.

Rate yourself from 1 (rarely) to 5 (consistently).

1. I give clear, structured opportunities for my team to assist me. _____
2. I provide feedback that builds confidence and skill. _____
3. I allow space for struggle without rushing to fix things. _____
4. I balance encouragement with challenge. _____
5. I see my team taking more initiative over time. _____

Score Key

21–25:	You're leading like a Sherpa—well done. Keep coaching and releasing.
16–20:	Good progress. Fine-tune your support and stretch strategies.
11–15:	Mixed signals—your team may need more guidance or safety.
10 or below:	Your team may be stuck. Reassess where you're over- or under engaging.

Practical Steps for Leaders

Development in the Immersion Stage is where coaching really starts. Use the next four steps to create momentum without overwhelming your team.

Call Out the Stage

Let team members know: "This is the part where it gets hard." Naming the struggle helps normalize it and builds resilience.

Instead of simply saying "This might be challenging," try: "Sarah, as you start learning our customer management system, you'll likely feel overwhelmed by all the different functions. That's completely normal—everyone goes through that phase. I struggled with the same thing when I learned it. Let's start with just the contact entry process, and I'll guide you through it step by step. We'll build on that foundation as you get comfortable."

Tailor the Feedback

Speak their Voice language. What motivates a Guardian won't work for a Connector. Adjust your coaching so it lands.

For a **Nurturer.** "The way you helped the team understand these changes shows your natural ability to support others. As you continue learning this process, remember that your development directly benefits everyone around you—they're counting on your insight to help them navigate this transition too."

For a **Creative.** "I can see you're starting to connect the dots between these individual tasks and our larger mission. Your unique perspective on this project could transform how we approach it. Let's explore how these technical details support the innovative direction you envisioned earlier."

For a **Guardian.** "I noticed how precisely you followed the first three steps of the process. That attention to detail is exactly what we need. For the next section, here's a checklist that will help you maintain that same level of accuracy."

For a **Connector.** "The energy you brought to the team training session made a huge difference in everyone's engagement. For our next phase, let's pair you with Jaime to work through these new procedures—you'll learn faster together, and I'd love to hear what improvements you both come up with for the client experience."

For a **Pioneer.** "You've already gotten farther with this than most people do in their first week. I'd like to challenge you to master the reporting feature by Friday—it's tricky, but I think you can beat my learning curve."

Normalize the Mess

Share your own stories of struggle and learning. Doing so creates safety and reminds your team that no one gets it perfect the first time.

When team members make their first significant mistake, be ready with a story like: "When I first ran this monthly report, I accidentally sent the unfiltered version to the entire executive team—including confidential salary data. It was mortifying, but it taught me to always double-check recipient lists and preview final outputs. That mistake made me much more careful and actually improved my process. What can we learn from this experience that will make you stronger?"

Celebrate Small Wins

Don't wait for big breakthroughs. Recognize progress, improvement, and effort—even when the results aren't flawless.

Instead of waiting for project completion, note incremental improvements: "I noticed you handled that client objection much more confidently than last week. You addressed their concern directly and offered a solution without needing my input. That's exactly the kind of progress that builds toward mastery."

Be specific about what team members did well and connect it to their growth journey: "The way you organized that spreadsheet shows you're developing a system-level understanding of our data structure. Three weeks ago, you were asking where to input the numbers; now you're designing efficient templates."

Leader's Challenge

The Immersion Stage is where your influence shifts—from doing the work to developing the people. It's where real leadership begins.

- Choose a task that someone on your team is ready to help with. It should stretch them, but not overwhelm them.
- Walk the team member through the task. Model how you do it, explain your thinking, and let them assist.
- Coach in real time. Don't jump in too quickly. Ask questions, provide guidance, and let them wrestle with it.
- Debrief afterward. Ask:
  - "What did you notice?"
  - "What challenged you?"
  - "What's one thing you'd do differently next time?"
- Watch for signs of progress. Initiative. Better questions. Confidence. That's how you know you're leading well.

Coaching starts when you slow down enough to build someone else's speed.

Now let's learn how to help people avoid the Pit of Despair.

8 | Avoiding the Pit of Despair

Helping Your People Win

Most people don't quit because they stop caring. They quit because they stop believing they can win.

It happens quietly at first—a hesitation before speaking up in a meeting, a task that sits unfinished a bit longer than usual, or a spark of enthusiasm that dims with each passing day. Then comes the inevitable question: "Am I even good at this?" And the slide begins.

By the time most leaders notice these subtle shifts, their team member has already begun the descent into what we call the Pit of Despair—that critical moment where confidence collapses and potential gets buried under doubt.

This chapter isn't just about recognizing these warning signs. It's about developing the leadership instincts to spot them early, the practical tools to intervene effectively, and the wisdom to know exactly what each voice type needs to stay out of the Pit.

Because the difference between a team member who gives up and one who breaks through often comes down to one factor: a leader who knows how to catch them before they fall.

The Reality with Developing People

Not everyone makes it.

That's the hard truth about developing people.

You start with good intentions—you teach, coach, and empower. But somewhere between the Immersion Stage (I Do, You Help) and the Empowerment Stage (You Do, I Help), people realize how hard it is to actually do what they've been tasked to do.

Team members who were once confident and eager suddenly become hesitant. They second-guess their decisions, withdraw in meetings, and stop taking initiative. What once looked like a promising employee in the making now seems stuck, frustrated, or completely disengaged.

This is the Pit of Despair—the moment when people realize just how much they don't know, how difficult the work actually is, and how far they still have to go. Many stop moving forward and settle into hiding and escaping at work instead of pressing forward.

Some get through it. Others don't.

The best leaders don't develop people just when it's easy; they help them avoid the Pit altogether.

What the Pit of Despair Actually Is

The employees' honeymoon phase of learning is over.

They have gone from Unconscious Incompetence (not knowing what they don't know) to Conscious Incompetence (painfully aware of their gaps). And it hurts.

They don't want to be seen as incompetent.

No one likes feeling embarrassed or unsure of themselves. If they can hide their struggles, maybe—just maybe—they won't have to face them. And so, instead of asking for help, they start retreating, avoiding challenges, and fall squarely into the Pit.

The Pit of Despair is the point in the learning process where a person's confidence crashes. It's the emotional and psychological low that happens when someone moves from observation to execution and suddenly realizes how difficult the skill or role actually is.

What seemed simple in theory becomes overwhelming in practice. The Pit is not just a struggle; it's a crisis of confidence.

- For high achievers, this moment can be crushing. They're used to being competent, and struggling makes them question their abilities.
- For perfectionists, the Pit is paralyzing. They want to get everything right, but now they're making mistakes they can't hide.
- For people who avoid failure, the Pit is dangerous. They would rather withdraw than risk looking incompetent.

The worst-case scenario? Instead of pushing through, they stop trying. Instead of fighting for growth, they settle—doing the bare minimum, avoiding challenges, and disengaging from development.

This is why leaders must step in before employees fall into the Pit.

Why People Get Stuck in the Pit

Once people fall into the Pit of Despair, it's incredibly difficult to climb out on their own. They get stuck because:

- They stop believing they can improve. The struggle feels endless, and they start thinking "Maybe I'm just not good at this."
- They don't want to be seen as incompetent. Rather than admit they're struggling, they hide it—hoping no one notices.
- They blame the leader. Instead of seeing the challenge as a part of growth, they start resenting the person who put them in the situation.

If left unchecked, the Pit of Despair becomes their permanent home—where people who have the potential to grow become employees who just show up but never truly engage.

What the Pit Looks Like in Real Time

Michael just got promoted to sales manager. He's great at selling, and his team expects him to lead by example.

At first, he's confident. He's excited to coach his team, set new targets, and run meetings.

But then reality sets in.

His first team meeting falls flat. The team is disengaged, and his attempt at motivation doesn't land the way he hoped.

His first quarter numbers dip. He realizes that coaching is very different from selling, and he's not sure how to help under-performers.

His boss gives him tough feedback but not helpful support. Suddenly Michael is painfully aware of how much he still has to learn.

Doubt creeps in. He starts hesitating. He second-guesses his coaching advice, afraid of saying the wrong thing. He avoids difficult conversations with his team, worried he'll come across as inexperienced. He starts playing it safe, taking fewer risks and waiting for his boss to make decisions.

At first, his team assumes he's just adjusting. But as the weeks go by, they start noticing that Michael isn't stepping up. And this is when Michael's boss steps in—not in a helpful way.

This is the Pit of Despair—where a promising leader starts slipping, hesitating, and pulling back instead of pushing forward.

The Slide Toward the Pit of Despair

Falling into the Pit of Despair doesn't happen overnight. It's a slow, creeping descent that often goes unnoticed until the person is fully stuck. This graph shows how the slide occurs.

DANGER ZONE

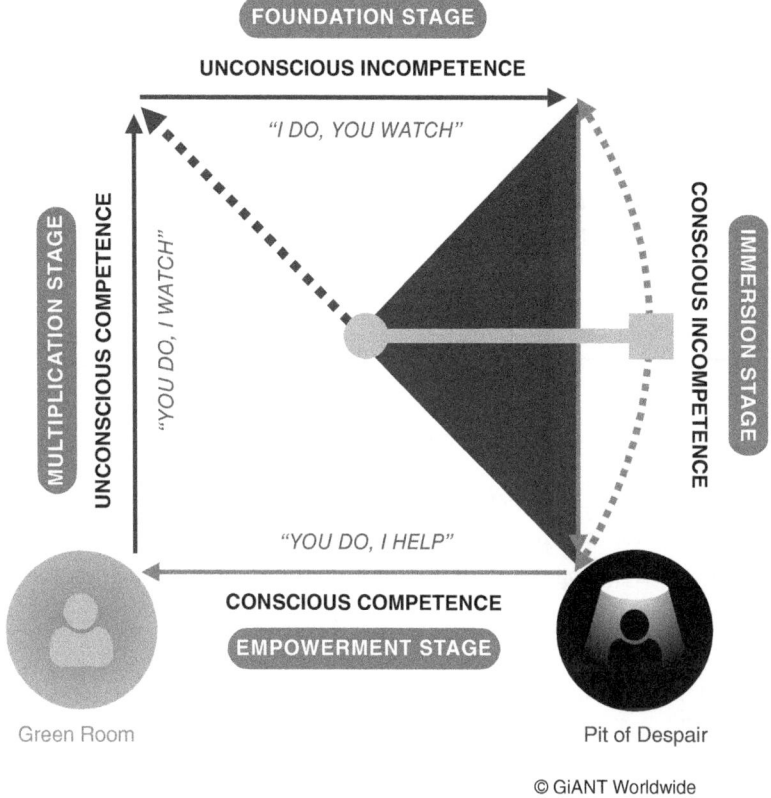

Green Room

Pit of Despair

© GiANT Worldwide

Source Credit: A. Maslow, Gordon Training International

Figure 8.1   Pit of Despair

The slide starts small. Employees:

- Hesitate on tasks they once tackled with confidence.
- Avoid challenges they used to find exciting.
- Overanalyze decisions and need constant reassurance.

At first, it looks like they just need a little extra support. But without intentional leadership, the slide becomes inevitable.

And when leaders don't step in?

These employees fall fully into the Pit of Despair, where learning stalls, stress takes over, and they begin to question whether they're even cut out for the role.

People don't quit because they stop caring. They quit because they feel unseen and unsupported.

Instead of thinking "I've got this, my boss believes in me," they start saying "Maybe I'm not good enough."

Instead of pushing through struggle, they start avoiding challenges altogether. And when they hit the pit? Most start blaming the person who put them there.

A Leader Who Didn't See the Pit Coming

Greg was one of the sharpest analysts in his department. He had a strong track record, sharp instincts, and was eager to prove himself.

So when his manager, Allison, saw an opportunity to elevate him, she gave him ownership of a high-stakes project.

At first, Greg was energized. He worked late, took charge, and seemed to be thriving. But as deadlines approached and pressure mounted, small mistakes crept in. Allison, busy with her own responsibilities, assumed Greg would figure it out—after all, he had always delivered before.

Then one day Greg missed a key deliverable.

Instead of admitting he was struggling, he avoided the conversation. When Allison finally checked in, he was defensive. He blamed unclear expectations, lack of support, and the unrealistic scope of the project.

By the time Allison realized Greg was in the Pit of Despair, he had already disengaged. He stopped taking initiative, avoided big decisions, and did just enough to get by.

What could have been a breakthrough moment for Greg turned into a confidence-crushing setback—all because Allison hadn't realized how much he was struggling.

She had assumed he was fine because he wasn't asking for help.

The reality is that Allison missed the Immersion Stage ("I do, you help") and assumed Greg was ready for the Empowerment Stage or even the Multiplication Stage.

Greg didn't want to admit he was drowning. He didn't want Allison to need to rescue him, but he did actually need help before he started giving up on himself.

Recognizing Trigger Points into the Pit of Despair

People don't fall into the Pit of Despair randomly. It's not just about stress or burnout—it's about encountering moments of incompetence that shake their confidence, especially when their leader isn't Voice-Driven and offering support with the challenge.

Each Voice offers specific clues—pain points that, when triggered, can push employees into the Pit of Despair faster than they, or their leaders, realize.

How Incompetence Affects Each Voice

The next table shows how incompetence affects people by Voice.

Learning to recognize the warning signs and intervene before someone slips into the Pit of Despair is vital for every team leader, parent, or mentor. When you stay attuned to employees' struggles and offer the right balance of support and challenge, you can help them push through, often avoiding the Pit altogether.

How to Keep People Out of the Pit of Despair

Reaching Conscious Competence means someone has observed, learned, and applied what they've been taught. It takes months—sometimes years—to build true skill and confidence.

The best leaders don't just hope their people figure it out. They actively prevent the slide toward the Pit of Despair by knowing exactly

Table 8.1   How Incompetence Affects Each Voice

Voice	What They Struggle With	What Triggers the Pit
Nurturer	Doubting competence when faced with hard decisions or conflict	Leader doesn't create emotional safety or reinforce their value before giving feedback
Creative	Struggling to simplify ideas or communicate them in a way that gains traction	Leader fails to validate their ideas or connect the vision to practical next steps
Guardian	Feeling overwhelmed when thrown into ambiguity or forced to act without a plan	Leader skips structure, changes expectations frequently, or dismisses their need for clarity
Connector	Losing confidence when they can't rally people or get buy-in for a vision	Leader ignores their need for relational connection or fails to show how the work impacts others
Pioneer	Feeling out of control when their skills don't immediately translate to success	Leader micromanages or slows them down without offering strategic challenges or clear goals

when to step in. They recognize when the teammate is at risk and learn how to provide the right amount of support at the right time.

The best leaders don't just develop people; they protect them from the Pit before they fall in.

The greatest mistake leaders make?

Thinking that silence means everything is okay.

Most people won't raise their hand and admit they're struggling. They'll just keep their head down, doing their best until they quietly disengage.

Three Essential Elements to Helping People Avoid the Pit of Despair

When a team member stands at the edge of the Pit of Despair, three critical elements make the difference between their growth and their collapse: Time, Vision, and Encouragement. (See Figure 8.2.) These aren't just nice-to-have leadership practices; they're the nonnegotiable foundation that keeps people moving forward when everything inside them wants to quit.

Let's examine how each element works and why it matters in the critical transition from watching to doing.

Time: The Fuel for Development

Time is the most valuable investment leaders can make in their people. Skill development, confidence building, and leadership growth don't happen overnight. Without enough structured and relational time, employees can feel unsupported and overwhelmed and may ultimately disengage before they ever reach competence.

Why Time Matters in Avoiding the Pit   The transition from watching to doing is where most employees struggle. At first, they're excited and overconfident, but as reality sets in, they recognize the gap

PIT OF DESPAIR

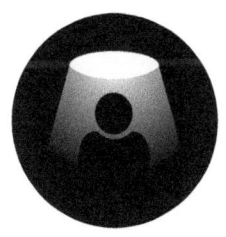

How to Help People Avoid the Pit of Despair:

▸ **Time:** Informal & Formal

▸ **Vision:** Short Term & Long Term

▸ **Encouragement:** Specific, Not Generic

Figure 8.2   Pit of Despair

between what they thought they knew and what they actually need to do. This is the moment where leadership matters most.

Leaders who fail to provide the right kind of time—both formal and informal—risk letting employees slip into discouragement. Those who invest time intentionally help their people push through uncertainty and build real competence.

Two Types of Time That Keep People Out of the Pit   **Formal time** is intentional, scheduled, and structured time for coaching and training. It includes coaching sessions, skill-building programs, and one-on-one development conversations. This is where leaders provide the guidance, feedback, and accountability team members need to grow with clarity and confidence.

What formal development time looks like.

- Weekly or biweekly one-on-one coaching sessions
- Scheduled development reviews tied to specific goals or benchmarks
- Structured onboarding or training programs for new skills
- Documented feedback loops with action steps and follow-up
- Leadership development workshops or learning tracks

Why it matters. Without formal coaching time, employees feel like they're being left to figure things out on their own. They may assume their struggles mean they're failing—when, in reality, they just need coaching. Formal development builds trust and creates a clear path toward growth.

How to implement it. Create recurring check-ins dedicated to development, not just performance updates. Use these meetings to review progress, set learning goals, and provide meaningful feedback. Make skill building part of the rhythm of work, not a side project.

Informal time consists of quick, spontaneous interactions— the small moments that reinforce learning and create a sense of psychological safety. These unscheduled daily check-ins and moments of encouragement help employees stay motivated and feel seen.

What informal development time looks like.

- A leader stopping by an employee's desk after a meeting to provide encouraging feedback
- A quick word of affirmation during a break or in the hallway
- A thoughtful message after a presentation or a tough moment
- An invitation to grab coffee or lunch—not as a reward but as a relational investment
- A relaxed conversation where the focus isn't performance but encouragement: "I'm for you. I believe in you. You've got what it takes."

Why it matters. Small, relational gestures send a powerful message: I see you. I'm with you. I believe in you. When people know they are supported beyond the task, they stay more engaged and confident, even during the hardest parts of the learning process.

How to implement it. Be present. Make a habit of asking "How's it going?" and mean it. Look for moments to recognize progress and offer encouragement in real time. Invest relationally, not just professionally.

The Science Behind the Pit of Despair People often start a new role or skill with enthusiasm, only to see their confidence drop a few weeks later. This is not a coincidence—it is a well-documented psychological pattern known as the Dunning-Kruger effect.[1]

When people begin learning a new skill, their initial excitement makes them feel overconfident because they do not yet understand the complexity of the task. But as they gain more exposure, they suddenly become aware of how much they do not know. Confidence drops before competence rises.

---

[1] Kruger, J. and Dunning, D. (1999). Unskilled and unaware of it: how difficulties in recognizing one's own incompetence lead to inflated self-assessments. *Journal of Personality and Social Psychology* 77 (6): 1121–1134.

This is where leaders are most needed. The Pit of Despair is where people feel vulnerable—questioning their abilities, second-guessing their choices, and fearing failure.

The leader is the most important variable to helping someone avoid the Pit by providing consistent time to help the employee avoid the Pit altogether.

How to Keep Them Out of the Pit with Time

- **Normalize the Learning Curve.** Say: — "This stage is tough for everyone. Struggle means you're learning, not failing."
- **Reinforce Small Wins.** Ask: "Remember when this was overwhelming for you? Look at what you've already mastered."
- **Give Targeted Support Without Taking Over.** Remember: Guide, don't rescue. Ask: "What's your next step?" instead of fixing the problem for employees.

The Leader's Challenge. Consider these questions to be an effective leader:

- Are you giving both structured learning time and relational time to struggling employees?
- Do you provide daily encouragement to reinforce effort and growth?
- Are you patient enough to let development take its natural course?

Vision: Reconnecting Today's Effort to Tomorrow's Promise

Vision is the antidote to discouragement. When someone begins to slide, the future starts to blur. The weight of today's struggles overshadows the progress they've made. Instead of seeing how far they've come, they question whether they're cut out for the journey at all.

That's when leaders must step in—not just to provide direction but to remind employees why they started in the first place.

Vision isn't just about casting strategy; it's about restoring belief. It's helping people see what's possible again. It's reminding them that mastery is on the other side of this hard moment. And most important, it's letting them borrow your belief until they rediscover their own.

The Vision Continuum

- **Short-term vision** brings clarity and focus to the immediate. "Here's what needs to happen this week—and why it matters."
- **Long-term vision** connects the struggle to something meaningful. "Here's where you're going. Imagine what it will feel like when you've mastered this."

Your role as a leader is to break through the fog.

When fear, insecurity, and frustration cloud employees' perspective, your job is to help them hope again. Remind them of their original "why." Paint a picture of what success will look and feel like. And above all, let them know you believe in their future.

Sometimes the most powerful thing a leader can say is "I see where you're going, and I still believe you can get there."

The Science of Hope and Vision When someone enters the Pit of Despair, they're not just facing a skill gap; they're facing a hope gap, which affects their vision of the future.

Hope, as defined by Dr. Chan Hellman, is not just a feeling—it's a measurable, cognitive process that fuels perseverance.[2] His research shows that hope is built through three core components:

1. **A clear goal.** A meaningful destination to aim for
2. **A realistic pathway.** A believable route to get there
3. **A sense of agency.** The belief that "I can take steps toward progress."

---

[2] Gwinn, C. and Hellman, C. (2018). *Hope Rising: How the Science of Hope Can Change Your Life*. Morgan James Publishing.

When one of these components is missing—especially for someone locked in the emotional weight of the Pit of Despair—people lose sight of the journey and begin to doubt if they belong. That's when leaders must intervene—not just with encouragement but with targeted, Voice-Driven guidance that speaks to how each person regains hope.

How Each Voice Rebuilds Hope

- **Nurturers** regain hope when they feel emotionally safe and reminded of the difference their work makes in the lives of others. "I know this is hard, but the way you support the team is irreplaceable. We need you."
- **Creatives** regain hope when they're shown that the long-term vision still exists, even if progress feels slow. "Your ideas still matter. Let's talk through how this tough season fits into the bigger story."
- **Guardians** regain hope when they can see a clear plan and logical next steps to move forward. "Here's a process that works. Let's walk through it one step at a time."
- **Connectors** regain hope when they are relationally reengaged and reminded of how their energy can influence and inspire others. "This moment doesn't define you. You bring life to this team. Let's get back in the game together."
- **Pioneers** regain hope when they are reconnected to the challenge and reminded that adversity is part of winning. "You're built for this. Let's reframe the goal and attack it with a smarter approach."

Leaders must learn to identify what hope looks like for each Voice. It's not one-size-fits-all encouragement. It's translating belief into a language they can hear, believe, and act on. Without that translation, even your best team members can lose their way.

The Voice-Driven leader knows that hope isn't wishful thinking; it's a strategic leadership trait to keep people out of the Pit.

How Leaders Can Restore Vision During Skill Mastery When a team member is stuck between the Immersion Stage and the Empowerment Stage, the Pit of Despair looms large. When an employee is straddling the Pit, it becomes very difficult to develop people because while the effort is high, their confidence is low. Progress feels invisible, and, without intentional support, the person may give up before the breakthrough.

This is where Voice-Driven leaders must reignite vision—not in a vague, motivational sense but in a practical, individualized way that restores clarity, hope, and momentum.

Rebuilding Vision Here is how to Rebuild Vision when a person is hovering around the Pit of Despair:

1. **Make Mastery Tangible.** Help people see what success will look and feel like once they reach conscious competence. Paint a picture of what they'll be capable of. "In two months, you'll be able to handle these meetings without me. You'll own it— and that's going to feel amazing."

2. **Connect Skill to Impact.** Remind them why this competency matters—to them, to the team, and to the mission. The Pit often feels isolating. Reconnect them to purpose. "When you get this down, it's going to take pressure off the whole team—and open new doors for you."

3. **Celebrate Grit, Not Just Outcomes.** In the Immersion Stage, even small progress is a big deal. Encourage effort. Acknowledge team members' resilience. Let them know you see them pushing through. "You may not feel it yet, but your reps are working. You're farther along than you think."

Leader's Insight. This is where development gets personal. Each person on your team is working their way around their own square. They need different types of vision and belief, delivered in the language they trust most.

People need to believe that the future can be better than today—and that they have the power to make it so.

Here are some example causes of the Pit of Despair:

- The goal seems unattainable.
- The path has become unclear.
- People no longer believe in themselves.

As a leader, your job is to restore vision. Not with abstract hype but with clear direction, Voice-specific encouragement, and belief that this stage will pass.

Leader's Challenge. Which of these questions do you need to focus on?

- Are you making Conscious Competence feel worth the struggle?
- Have you connected the skill they're learning to real impact?
- Can they say that you believe in them, even when they're doubting themselves?

Encouragement: Being Specific, Genuine, and Personal

Encouragement isn't about throwing around generic praise; it's about targeted affirmation that rebuilds confidence when people need it most. When under pressure, people begin doubting their abilities, questioning whether they belong, and assuming their struggles mean they're failing.

At that moment, your belief in them must be stronger than their doubt. The right words at the right time can be the difference between someone pressing forward or pulling back.

- **Specific Encouragement.** Vague praise like "Good job" doesn't cut it. Instead, say: "I saw the way you handled that tough conversation today—you stayed calm, asked great questions, and got to a resolution."

- **Genuine Encouragement.** People can sense empty words. Encouragement must be tied to real progress and effort, not just an automatic compliment.
- **Personal Encouragement.** Know what matters to each person. People want to be known, and when you are personal and specific, you give them words that become fuel that they will need to keep people out of the Pit of Despair.

The Science and Faith Behind Encouragement as Belief Encouragement is not just about making people feel better; it is about instilling belief in someone when they can't see their own potential. Both science and faith traditions affirm that belief, when reinforced through encouragement, has the power to change behavior, rewire thought patterns, and even shape destiny.

The Neuroscience of Encouragement and Belief Encouragement has a direct impact on the brain. Research shows that when people receive positive reinforcement, their brain releases dopamine—the chemical that boosts motivation, focus, and confidence.[3] This chemical reaction makes it easier for people to push through challenges and reinforces behaviors that lead to success.

Encouragement is more than feeling good. Encouragement changes how people interpret failure. According to cognitive reframing theory, when people receive timely, specific encouragement, they start seeing struggles as part of the learning process rather than as signs of incompetence.[4] This shift in mindset is what separates those who keep going from those who give up.

When people consistently receive encouragement, their brain literally rewires itself to expect success rather than failure. The words of

---

[3] Berridge, K.C. and Robinson, T.E. (1998). What is the role of dopamine in reward: hedonic impact, reward learning, or incentive salience? *Brain Research Reviews* 28(3): 309–369.
[4] Beck, A.T. (1967). *Depression: Clinical, Experimental, and Theoretical Aspects.* University of Pennsylvania Press.

a leader, mentor, or coach become the internal dialogue a person uses to navigate future challenges.

The Faith Component: The Power of Spoken Belief   Faith traditions have long recognized the power of belief spoken over a person's life. The Bible, for instance, emphasizes the transformative power of words with Proverbs 18:21 saying "The tongue has the power of life and death."

In other words, belief doesn't just arise on its own—it is spoken, reinforced, and nurtured. Encouragement functions in the same way. Leaders, parents, and mentors who consistently affirm someone's abilities are doing more than just making them feel good; they are shaping the person's long-term confidence and performance.

Encouragement as a Leadership Tool   Encouragement isn't soft; it's strategic. Especially when team members are navigating the Pit of Despair. Encouragement becomes the fuel that keeps people moving when everything inside them wants to quit.

Moving from the Immersion Stage to the Engagement Stage is the hardest part of growth. People know what to do, but they're not yet doing it consistently. They feel exposed, frustrated, and behind. Confidence is shaky. Progress feels slow. That's when a Voice-Driven leader steps in—not with vague positivity but with grounded belief and a steady presence.

Encouragement in this moment sounds like: "You can do this. I've seen this before. I've been there myself. Trust me—don't give up on yourself now. We're going to get through this together."

To be a Voice-Driven leader, your encouragement must be:

- **Specific.** Acknowledge the effort, not just the outcome: "That meeting didn't go perfectly, but you stayed composed and asked great follow-up questions. That's a win."
- **Grounded in Belief.** Speak to who they're becoming, not just what they've done: "This is the messy middle. It's not pretty, but this is where leaders are made."

- **Personal.** Let them borrow your confidence until they find their own: "I wouldn't be investing this time if I didn't believe in you. You've got what it takes."

Encouragement isn't flattery—it's leadership presence in its purest form. It's saying: "You don't have to believe fully in yourself yet. I'll hold that belief for both of us until you do."

> *In their hardest moment, your belief might be the only thing holding them up.*

Voice-Specific Frameworks for Avoiding the Pit of Despair

The best leaders don't just help people out of the Pit of Despair; they help them avoid it altogether. All team members have different triggers that can cause them to lose confidence and disengage, but with the right approach, you can keep them moving forward before they ever get stuck.

To do this, leaders must provide the right balance of time, vision, and encouragement in ways that resonate with each of the 5 Voices. Here's how to lead proactively and prevent your people from slipping into the Pit.

Nurturer: "Do I Really Matter Here?"

Here are the warning signs for a Nurturer near the Pit of Despair:

- Quieter than usual in meetings or team discussions
- Increased concern about how changes impact others
- Self-doubt expressed through excessive apologizing
- Withdrawal from offering opinions or perspectives
- Taking on extra work to avoid "disappointing" the team
- Emotional distance where warmth previously existed

Leader's Response: Time, Vision, Encouragement TIME: Build relational trust before correction. Nurturers need emotional safety before they can embrace growth challenges. Without relational time, they'll retreat further into self-doubt.

- **Formal Relational Time.** Begin development conversations with personal check-ins before diving into performance feedback. Create a judgment-free zone for questions.
- **Informal Relational Time.** Make space for brief, authentic connection. Ask "How are you really doing with this transition?" and listen fully before offering guidance.

VISION: Connect their growth to team well-being. For Nurturers, personal development must link directly to how it helps others. Show them that mastering skills isn't selfish; it's essential for the team's success.

- **Short-term Vision.** "As you get comfortable with this process, you'll be able to create a more supportive environment for new team members."
- **Long-term Vision.** "Your growth in this area will enable you to care for the team in ways no one else can."

ENCOURAGEMENT: Affirm their value and impact. Nurturers often discount their contributions. During the struggle of the Immersion Stage, they need specific affirmation of how their unique strengths matter.

- **Be Specific.** "The way you noticed Maria struggling and helped her understand the process shows your remarkable awareness."
- **Reinforce Identity.** "Your thoughtfulness creates safety that allows this entire team to take risks and grow."

Putting Development into Practice When Rachel, a Nurturer HR specialist, began withdrawing during a difficult system implementation, her leader recognized the early signs. Instead of pushing for faster progress, she invited Rachel to coffee and said: "I've noticed you seem concerned about this transition. Before we dive into the technical details, I want you to know that your care for our people is exactly why I need your help with this. The empathy you bring ensures we don't lose the human element in all these changes."

By connecting Rachel's growth to her core value of supporting others, the leader helped Rachel see that mastering the new system wasn't just about technical skill; it was about enhancing her ability to care for the team in even more meaningful ways.

Creative: "Does My Voice Even Matter Here?"

Here are the warning signs for a Creative near the Pit of Despair:

- Disengagement from detailed tasks or structured processes
- Increased frustration when ideas aren't understood or implemented
- Withdrawal into abstract thinking without practical application
- Resistance to following established procedures or templates
- Growing cynicism about the organization's openness to innovation
- Tendency to work alone rather than collaborate within constraints

Leader's Response: Time, Vision, Encouragement TIME: Balance structure with space for processing. Creatives need both clear direction and room to connect ideas. In the Immersion Stage, they require structure that doesn't stifle their natural thought process.

- **Formal Time.** Start with big-picture context before diving into steps. Create visual roadmaps that show both the process and its purpose.
- **Informal Time.** Allow short thinking breaks during learning. Ask: "What connections are you seeing that we might be missing?"

VISION: Link mastery to future innovation opportunity. Show how current skill building enables greater creative impact later. Help them see structure as a foundation for innovation, not a constraint.

- **Short-term Vision.** "Once you understand how this system works, you'll see opportunities to improve it that no one else will notice."
- **Long-term Vision.** "Mastering these fundamentals will give your ideas the credibility and framework they need to transform how we approach this entire area."

ENCOURAGEMENT: Validate their unique perspective. Creatives need to know their different viewpoint is valued. When struggling with details, they need affirmation that their conceptual strengths remain important.

- **Be Specific.** "That question you asked in the meeting challenged our assumptions in exactly the right way."
- **Reinforce Identity.** "Your ability to see possibilities others miss is why we need you to master this—so your vision can actually be implemented."

Putting Development into Practice   When Alex, a Creative marketing specialist, became visibly frustrated learning campaign analytics, his leader noticed his increasing detachment. Rather than just emphasizing the technical requirements, she said: "Alex, I know these spreadsheets seem disconnected from the creative work you excel at. But here's why this matters: Once you understand how to read this data, you'll be able to prove which of your creative concepts actually resonates most with our audience. This isn't about turning you into an analyst—it's about giving your creative brilliance the evidence it needs to drive our strategy."

By reframing the technical learning as an amplifier for his creative impact rather than as a restriction, his leader helped Alex reconnect with the purpose behind the process and push through the challenging learning curve.

Guardian: "*Why Does Everything Feel So Chaotic?*"

Here are the warning signs for a Guardian near the Pit of Despair:

- Increased questions about process details or requirements
- Hesitation to move forward without complete information
- Growing frustration with changing priorities or unclear expectations
- Withdrawal from collaborative settings where decisions feel rushed
- Excessive documentation as an attempt to create missing structure
- Rigid adherence to established procedures even when flexibility is needed

Leader's Response: Time, Vision, Encouragement TIME: Offer predictable, process-oriented coaching. Guardians don't just need feedback; they need a map. In the Immersion Stage, regular, structured check-ins provide the clarity they crave and prevent them from spiraling when things feel out of control.

- **Formal Time.** Set up a development roadmap. Break the skill down into steps and milestones. Use checklists or templates when possible.
- **Informal Time.** Ask precision-oriented questions like: "Is anything unclear to you right now?" or "What part of this feels disorganized?"

VISION: Translate ambiguity into structure. For Guardians, vision must be concrete and operational. The goal isn't to inspire them; it's to reduce their uncertainty. If they can see how the task fits into the system, they'll reengage quickly.

- **Short-term Vision.** "Here's what success looks like this week. Let's eliminate the noise."

- **Long-term Vision.** "Once this becomes second nature, you'll be the one designing the system for others."

ENCOURAGEMENT: Recognize precision and consistency. Guardians rarely seek attention, so it's easy to overlook their quiet contributions. But during the hard slog of the Immersion Stage, they need encouragement that acknowledges their discipline, not just their outcomes.

- **Be Specific.** "The way you documented that process saved us hours this week."
- **Reinforce Identity.** "Your attention to detail is exactly what makes this work sustainable."

Putting Development into Practice   When Ellen, a Guardian analyst, became increasingly hesitant during a systems rollout, her leader noticed the early warning signs. Instead of pushing harder, he said: "I can tell the process isn't feeling solid yet. Let's walk through each step together, then I'll show you how this fits into our wider ops plan."

By providing structure, clarity, and recognition of her need for order, her leader kept Ellen from slipping into the Pit and instead helped her build confidence through methodical mastery.

Connector: "Why Does This Feel So Boring or Disconnected?"

Here are the warning signs for a Connector near the Pit of Despair:

- Decreased energy and enthusiasm in meetings or training sessions
- Shift from relationship building to just completing tasks
- Reduced engagement with team members
- Questions focusing on "when will this be over" rather than content
- Struggling to see how technical details connect to people impact
- Increased impatience with processes that feel isolating or repetitive

Leader's Response: Time, Vision, Encouragement TIME: Create interactive, energizing development. Connectors need engagement, not just instruction. When learning feels isolated or monotonous, they begin to disengage and lose their natural spark.

- **Formal Time.** Build peer learning opportunities and discussion into development. Keep sessions interactive and varied with quick-paced activities.
- **Informal Time.** Check in with energy-focused questions: "What parts of this process are draining your enthusiasm?" or "How can we make this more engaging?"

VISION: Connect tasks to people and relationships. Show how mastering skills creates relationship opportunities. Connectors need to see how technical competence enhances their ability to influence and bring people together.

- **Short-term Vision.** "Once you're comfortable with this system, you'll be able to focus completely on the client instead of worrying about the process."
- **Long-term Vision.** "Mastering this will position you as the go-to person who can bridge between our technical teams and stakeholders."

ENCOURAGEMENT: Fuel their energy and relational impact. Connectors thrive on knowing their enthusiasm matters. When pushing through Immersion Stage challenges, they need affirmation that their relational gifts remain valuable.

- **Be Specific:** "The way you brought everyone together for that solution showed your unique ability to create collaboration."
- **Reinforce Identity:** "Your energy shifts the entire room. As you master these skills, that influence will only grow stronger."

Putting Development into Practice   When Sophia, a Connector account manager, began losing her characteristic enthusiasm during customer relationship management training, her leader didn't just focus on the technical requirements. Instead, she said: "Let's try something different. I'd like you and James to work together on the next module and find three ways this system could help you personalize client interactions. Your ability to make technology feel human is exactly what will set our service apart."

By reframing technical learning as a tool for relationship building and creating a more social learning experience, her leader rekindled Sophia's natural energy and helped her see how mastery would enhance her greatest strength: connecting with people.

Pioneer: "Why Am I Not Winning at This Yet?"

Here are the warning signs for a Pioneer near the Pit of Despair:

- Increased impatience with the learning process
- Pushing too hard then pulling back when quick mastery doesn't happen
- Growing frustration with detailed instruction or methodical approaches
- Tendency to blame tools, processes, or others for lack of progress
- Comparing their learning curve to past successes in other areas
- Taking shortcuts that undermine skill development to appear competent

Leader's Response: Time, Vision, Encouragement   TIME: Provide direct, results-focused coaching. Pioneers need efficiency and challenge, not hand holding. They want coaching that feels like forward momentum, not endless processing.

- **Formal Time.** Keep development sessions brief, high-impact, and focused on measurable progress. Create clear benchmarks to track advancement.

- **Informal Time.** Use quick check-ins that highlight improvement: "You're 80% there—let's lock in that last 20% this week."

VISION: Frame the struggle as part of the victory. Show how the current challenge is preparing them for bigger impact. Pioneers need to see that temporary struggle leads to greater influence and opportunity.

- **Short-term Vision.** "Pushing through this learning curve faster than others will put you ahead of the competition."
- **Long-term Vision.** "Mastering this now will qualify you to lead the expansion project we're planning next quarter."

ENCOURAGEMENT: Challenge wrapped in confidence. Pioneers don't want comfort; they want to be pushed while knowing you believe in their capacity to win. Encouragement must be both challenging and affirming.

- **Be Specific.** "You made more progress in three days than most people make in two weeks."
- **Reinforce Identity.** "This is exactly the kind of challenge you're built for. You're a finisher—and that's why I know you'll break through."

Putting Development into Practice When Ryan, a Pioneer sales manager, became visibly frustrated learning a complex new proposal system, his director recognized the warning signs of the Pit of Despair. Instead of offering reassurance, she leaned into his competitive nature: "Ryan, I know this feels tedious right now. But here's what I see: You're already ahead of where the East Coast team was at this point. If you can master this system by Friday, you'll be the first person I want leading the training for the rest of the division. This is the kind of technical edge that will separate top performers in our next promotion round."

Table 8.2   How to Keep Each Voice out of the Pit of Despair

Voice	Warning Signs	Time	Vision	Encouragement
Nurturer	Emotional withdrawal Contributes less in meetings Increased worry about impact on others	Relational connection before correction Safe space to process feelings	Show how their growth helps others Emphasize team impact	"The care you're putting into this makes a difference for everyone"
Creative	Disengagement from details Fixation on bigger ideas Frustration with structure	Big-picture context first, then structured steps Space to process ideas	Connect mundane tasks to innovation opportunity Show future influence	"Your perspective will transform this once you master the basics"
Guardian	Increased questions about process Hesitation without complete information Frustration with ambiguity	Clear checklists Structured feedback Step-by-step direction	Concrete roadmaps Eliminate unnecessary change Show how pieces connect	"Your attention to detail is keeping this project on track"
Connector	Reduced energy Less engagement with team Focus on transactional rather than relational work	Interactive learning Keep it energetic Build in social elements	Connect tasks to people impact Show relationship opportunities	"Your ability to bring people together is exactly what will make this successful"
Pioneer	Impatience with process Pushing too hard then pulling back Frustration with lack of quick wins	Brief, results-focused coaching Don't Waste Time	Frame struggle as part of winning Connect mastery to bigger opportunity	"You're built for this challenge; this resistance is making you stronger"

By framing the challenge as a competition with a clear reward for mastery, she rekindled Ryan's natural drive and helped him see the struggle as part of a winning strategy, not a sign of weakness.

> *Proactive attention is the difference between quiet quitting and courageous comeback.*

Quick Reference: Keeping Each Voice Out of the Pit

We believe in practical application, which is why we have built so many tables like this for you to refer to. Here is how to keep each Voice out of the Pit.

Helping People Who Have Already Fallen into the Pit

We've spent time discussing how to help people avoid the Pit of Despair, but what happens if someone you lead or inherited on your team has already fallen into the Pit?

How Does Each Voice Behave in the Pit of Despair?   One of the hardest realities in leadership is helping people who are stuck in the Pit of Despair.

When someone lingers in the bottom right corner of the Development Square without the right support, the result is more than frustration; it's disillusionment. What began as a confidence dip turns into withdrawal, mistrust, and, in some cases, open resistance. People stuck in the Pit of Despair aren't bad people; they're people who need belief, clarity, and support. The above table shows the behavior of each Voice in the Pit.

Reality for Leaders. If you're leading someone who's been stuck in the Pit, your job isn't to blame the past. It's to reintroduce belief, rebuild trust, and help them reenter the Development Square. You'll need more intentionality and more patience.

Who Is Responsible for Getting Someone Out of the Pit of Despair?   The Pit of Despair is rarely the fault of just one party; it is usually a shared responsibility between the leader and the employee.

Table 8.3   Behavior by Voice

Voice	Behavior When Left in the Pit	Impact on the Team
Nurturer	Withdraws Stops offering support Begins to feel invisible	Team morale drops Emotional cohesion disappears
Creative	Becomes cynical, overly critical, or shuts down	Innovation slows Strategic ideas vanish

Guardian	Doubles down on
	  control and rules
	Becomes inflexible
		Processes stall
		Communication feels
		  rigid and defensive

Connector	Begins passive-aggressive behavior or gossiping	Trust erodes Team culture fractures

Pioneer	Gets cold, detached, and
	  focuses only on
	  performance
		People feel used, not
		  valued
		Retention drops

Leaders set the tone for clarity, culture, and support. Some key questions leaders must ask themselves:

- Did I provide clear expectations? If the role is ambiguous, confusion and frustration will follow.
- Did I offer both support and challenge? If there is too much support without challenge, employees become complacent. If there is too much challenge without support, they become overwhelmed.
- Did I ensure the employee was equipped with the right tools, training, and resources? Voice-Driven leaders provide the support needed to do the job.
- Did I foster an environment where open communication and feedback are welcomed? Trust is crucial to employee growth.
- Have I checked in regularly to assess their engagement and mindset?

When Employees Are Ready to Reenter the Development Journey Getting stuck in the Pit of Despair is not the end; it's a time to reset. And while leaders play a significant role in guiding people out, employees must also choose to reengage.

Remember, no one can be developed without their consent. If you've been sitting in the Pit—frustrated, checked out, or quietly discouraged—the only way forward is to reenter the Development Square. That means starting back at the Foundation Stage, even if doing so feels like taking a step backward.

Here's what an employee must do to regain momentum:

- **Recommit to Learning (Foundation Stage).** Admit what you don't know. Let go of false confidence and be open to starting fresh. "I'm willing to watch, listen, and learn again—even if it's uncomfortable."
- **Embrace the Struggle (Immersion Stage).** Understand that growth requires friction. Mistakes don't mean failure; they mean progress. "I expect to struggle. I won't quit when things get hard."
- **Take Ownership (Empowerment Stage).** Begin doing the work yourself—with guidance. Trust the process and lean into feedback. "I'm ready to try, even if I still need help."

The Development Square is not a linear escalator; it's a tool for intentional growth. It's important for the leader and the team member to understand the past tendencies to fall into the Pit of Despair and adjust differently this time.

When employees understand where they are and recommit to the process, they can move from frustration to ownership and from self-doubt to self-leadership.

If you sense an employee is ready to reengage after time in the Pit, your job is to meet them at the Foundation Stage with no assumptions, no shame, just a clear invitation to start again.

The Shared Responsibility of Success   Ultimately, success is a partnership. Leaders must ensure they have done everything possible to set employees up for success while employees must take responsibility for their engagement and performance. The leader functions as a ladder out of the Pit, but the employee must be willing to climb.

When a team member falls into the Pit of Despair, they've moved from Naive Confidence into the hard reality of Conscious Incompetence. The excitement is gone. The learning curve is steep. The temptation to retreat or give up is real.

And this is where the leader matters most.

The leader becomes the **ladder** that helps them climb out of the Pit, not by pulling them out but by giving them the rungs they need to rise.

Here's how the five-rung ladder works.

Rung 1. Normalizing the Struggle   The leader says, *"You're not failing—you're learning. Everyone hits this wall."*

When someone feels stuck, their first need is perspective. By naming the Pit and normalizing the struggle, the leader breaks the cycle of self-doubt. Doing this creates psychological safety and renews the person's courage to keep trying.

Rung 2. Adjusting Support and Challenge   The leader calibrates their leadership:

- **High Support:** Encouragement, time, coaching, empathy.
- **High Challenge:** Clarity, standards, accountability.

Leading with support and challenge helps the team member regain confidence *without* removing responsibility. Leaders don't climb in and do the work; they steady the ladder and coach from the side.

Rung 3. Providing Practical Feedback   In the Pit, abstract encouragement isn't enough. To help the stuck team member, the leader gives Voice-specific, behavior-focused feedback:

- "Here's what you did well."
- "Here's where you're improving."
- "Here's what to try next."

This feedback turns confusion into clarity—and clarity fuels momentum.

Rung 4. Highlighting Progress   People in the Pit often forget how far they've come. The leader reminds them:

- "Remember when this used to scare you?"
- "Look how much faster you did that this time."
- "You're not where you want to be—but you're not where you were."

This rung builds belief—and belief helps people climb.

Rung 5. Recasting the Vision   Finally, the leader lifts the team member's eyes to what's ahead: *"This is all preparing you for the next level. What you're learning now is what will make you a leader others trust later."*

This rung renews purpose and shows the Pit isn't the end; it's a passage.

Without the ladder, people stay stuck. But with a leader who coaches through the Pit, team members develop resilience, self-awareness, and real skill.

Because in the end, great leaders don't carry people out of the Pit. **They build ladders—and help people climb.**

What Do I Do with a Resistant Employee in the Pit? Sometimes leaders inherit team members who have been left too long in the Pit of Despair. These individuals aren't just discouraged; they're stuck. And over time, they've either become responsive or resistant to development.

Responsive employees are still reachable. They're open to feedback, willing to reengage, and show signs of wanting to grow, even if they're uncertain or insecure. They may be in the Pit, but they're looking for a way out.

Resistant employees, however, have dug in. They've internalized struggle as failure, and they view any attempt at development as a threat. They push back against feedback, avoid new challenges, and stay rooted in their comfort zones. In some cases, they may appear checked out or passive-aggressive or may even undermine efforts to build a healthy team culture.

The key difference? **Mindset.**

Responsive employees still believe growth is possible. Resistant employees have stopped trying.

Here's the hard truth: No leader can drag someone out of the Pit who refuses to take a step.

How Great Leaders Handle Resistant Employees Resistant employees are hard. These are the people who tend to blame others or not accept responsibility for their actions. Here are some tips you can do to handle their resistance:

- **Extend the Invitation to Reengage.** Let them know the door to development is open, but they'll need to walk through it. They will have to start again at the Foundation Stage, with humility and a willingness to learn. "I know things haven't been easy, but I believe you still have a lot to contribute. If you're willing to reengage, I'll walk with you through the process."
- **Clarify the Path Forward.** Set clear expectations: What responsiveness looks like, what support you'll provide, and what

progress should be visible within a set time. "We'll start small. I'll be checking in weekly. If you're showing up and leaning in, I'll match your effort. But we can't stay where it is."

- **Set a Clear Timeline.** Rescue without boundaries becomes rescue without results. Resistant employees need to see the timeline, not just the opportunity. "You don't have to be perfect, but we need to see progress within the next 30 to 60 days. If not, we'll need to have a different conversation about your role on this team."

If a resistant employee refuses to reengage, the kindest, most effective thing you can do—for them and for your team—is to act.

Unchecked resistant behavior becomes contagious. It creates confusion, lowers morale, and damages the culture you're trying to build.

Great leaders give every opportunity for reengagement, but they do not let resistant behavior linger indefinitely.

> *The invitation to reengage is the leader's responsibility. The decision to respond is the employees.*

What Happens If Someone Self-Sabotages in the Pit of Despair? Self-sabotage is one of the most damaging behaviors in the Pit of Despair because it turns internal doubt into self-inflicted failure. When employees feel overwhelmed or unseen, they may unconsciously undermine themselves as a way to cope with stress or regain a false sense of control. Unchecked, this behavior can derail confidence, performance, and team trust.

Breaking the Cycle of Self-Sabotage There are three parts to the cycle of self-sabotage:

1. **Avoidance: Pulling Back Instead of Pushing Forward.** Some employees dodge discomfort by procrastinating, avoiding responsibility, or convincing themselves they never wanted success. Leaders may mistake this for a lack of motivation, reinforcing their fears.

Prevent self-sabotage by:

- Setting small, achievable goals to rebuild confidence.
- Increasing structured check-ins to maintain engagement.
- Helping them believe it's worth the effort and you are willing to help them.

2. **Defensiveness: Blaming Instead of Owning Growth.** Rather than facing challenges, some employees deflect feedback, blame leadership, or criticize the system. This isolates them from the support they need.

   Prevent defensiveness by:

   - Framing feedback as coaching, not criticism.
   - Asking reflective questions to build self-awareness.
   - Modeling ownership by sharing your own growth moments.

3. **Self-fulfilling Failure: Justifying Doubt Through Actions.** When employees feel helpless, they may miss deadlines, underperform, or withdraw, proving to themselves that they are not capable.

   Prevent self-fulfilling failure by:

   - Addressing small failures before they become patterns.
   - Reframing mistakes as learning, not evidence of incompetence.
   - Highlighting past resilience to shift their perspective.

Self-sabotage isn't proof of failure; it's a cry for help.

The Leader's Role in Stopping Self-Sabotage Self-sabotage thrives in silence. The best leaders step in early, speak belief over their people, and create structured support to keep them engaged. If someone stays in the Pit too long, doubt becomes their identity. Great leaders intervene before that happens.

When Should Someone Be Let Go?   Letting someone go is one of the hardest decisions a leader will make, but it is sometimes necessary for the health of both the individual and the organization. The goal of leadership is to develop people, not discard them at the first sign of struggle. However, when someone refuses to grow, resists accountability, or consistently undermines the team, keeping them in the role does more harm than good.

Here are key signs that someone may need to be let go:

- **Consistent Lack of Effort or Improvement.** Struggle is normal. Lack of progress is not. If employees receive coaching, time, and clear expectations but continues to underperform, it may be a sign they are unwilling or unable to meet the role's requirements.

  Leader's Question. Have I provided them with the tools, feedback, and support needed to succeed?

- **Repeated Resistance to Feedback.** Employees who are coachable will make adjustments over time. People who consistently reject feedback, become defensive, or refuse to take responsibility for mistakes are signaling that they are not willing to grow.

  Leader's Question. Have they shown any willingness to apply feedback and take ownership of their development?

- **Persistent Negative Impact on Team Culture.** One disengaged employee can lower morale, create drama, or slow down progress for the entire team. If people are consistently draining energy, spreading negativity, or damaging trust, their presence is costing more than their individual performance.

  Leader's Question. Is this person making the team stronger or holding the team back?

- **Lack of Alignment with Core Values.** Skills can be trained, but values must be lived. If employees continuously operate outside the company's core values—whether through unethical behavior, toxic communication, or disregard for team expectations—letting them stay sends the wrong message to the rest of the organization.

  Leader's Question. Does their behavior align with what we stand for as a team and organization?

- **They No Longer Care About the Work or the Mission.**
  When people have mentally checked out, they may stay in the
  role for a paycheck but contribute as little as possible. This disengagement affects their own job satisfaction and the energy of
  those around them.
  Leader's Question. Do they still care about the work or
  are they just showing up?

The Last Step Before Letting Someone Go   Before making the final
decision, ensure you have:

- Clearly communicated expectations and provided measurable
  benchmarks for improvement.
- Offered feedback, coaching, and opportunities for growth.
- Had direct conversations about the concerns and given them a
  chance to respond.
- Documented performance issues and past interventions.

If, after all this, people still refuse to engage, improve, or contribute positively, then letting them go is not a failure; it is an act of leadership. Sometimes the kindest thing you can do is release people from a
job they are not thriving in so they can find a better fit elsewhere.

*Please note that each organization has its own policies toward releasing employ-
ees. We recommend you follow your HR initiatives to ensure a proper dismissal.*

What to Do If You Inherit Someone in the Pit of Despair

Inheriting struggling team members is challenging. You didn't put
them there, but now it's your responsibility to assess whether they can
improve or if they've chosen to stay stuck. Here is how to deal with
the problem of inheriting someone in the Pit of Despair:

1. **Diagnose the Root Issue.** Not all employees in the Pit end up
   there for the same reason. Before assuming they're unmotivated,

take time to understand what led to their struggle. Ask yourself:

■ How long have they been struggling?

■ What caused the decline—poor leadership, unclear expectations, or lack of training?

■ Do they recognize their struggle, or have they given up?

If they don't acknowledge their situation, they may have already accepted being stuck, which is a red flag.

2. **Have a Direct But Supportive Conversation.** Once you've assessed the situation, address it openly. Your goal is to reset expectations and gauge their willingness to improve. Say:

■ "I see potential in you, but I also see you're stuck. Let's figure out how to move forward."

■ "What do you need to regain confidence and get back on track?"

If the person responds with blame or apathy, improvement is unlikely.

3. **Set a Short-term Plan for Progress.** If they are willing to improve, give them structured steps.

■ 30-day plan: Define clear, measurable goals.

■ Support: Offer training, coaching, and mentorship.

■ Real-time feedback: Correct mistakes and celebrate wins immediately.

■ Regular check-ins: Track progress and remove roadblocks.

People in the Pit need small wins to regain confidence. Without such wins, they may stay stuck.

4. **Watch for Progress or Resistance.** By now, you'll see either effort or excuses.

If the employee improves:

■ Reinforce small wins.

■ Gradually increase responsibility.

■ Help them transition into competence.

If the employee stays stuck:
- Be clear that stagnation is not an option.
- Start discussing an exit strategy if needed.

5. **Know When to Let Them Go.** Not everyone will make it out of the Pit of Despair. If you've provided time, training, and support but see no effort, it's time to move on.

Here are signs that it's time to let employees go:
- They reject feedback and resist change.
- They blame others instead of taking ownership.
- Their attitude is affecting the rest of the team.

Letting someone go isn't failure—it's making room for the right person. Keeping a disengaged employee in place harms both them and your team.

Bottom Line: Can You Get Employees Out of the Pit of Despair? Yes—if they're willing. But you can't force someone to take ownership of their growth.

The Truth About Getting Out of the Pit of Despair

Not everyone makes it out. Some will choose to stay stuck—blaming circumstances, rejecting help, or deciding the struggle isn't worth it. Others, with the right leadership and personal resilience, will push through and come out stronger.

A leader's job is to give them the tools, support, and belief they need to climb out themselves.

We can only do our part. Because when someone climbs out of the struggle stronger, they don't just regain their footing—they become better leaders themselves.

Great leaders do to others what they would want for themselves.

Preventing the Pit of Despair isn't just about managing performance; it's about shaping transformation. When you successfully guide people through their moments of doubt, you don't just keep them from falling; you help them discover a resilience they didn't know they had.

As we explore in the next chapter, true empowerment emerges when people stop doubting and start believing they have what it takes to lead. The Empowerment Stage is where your investment in keeping people out of the Pit pays its greatest dividends—as they step confidently into their leadership potential and begin the journey toward Multiplication.

9 | The Empowerment Stage

"You Do, I Help"

In Chapter 7, we explored how to navigate the Immersion Stage, where team members assist while you lead. This collaborative approach builds their competence as they learn alongside you. But development doesn't stop there. Once they've mastered the basics and survived the Pit of Despair, it's time for a critical shift—one that challenges both of you in new ways.

This chapter explores the critical third phase of leadership development—the Empowerment Stage—where the dynamic shifts from "I do, you help" to "You do, I help." (See Figure 9.1.) At this pivotal point, team members take primary responsibility while leaders transition to a supportive coaching role.

This stage represents the most challenging leadership transition for both parties: Leaders must resist the urge to either micromanage or

STAGE THREE: **EMPOWERMENT**

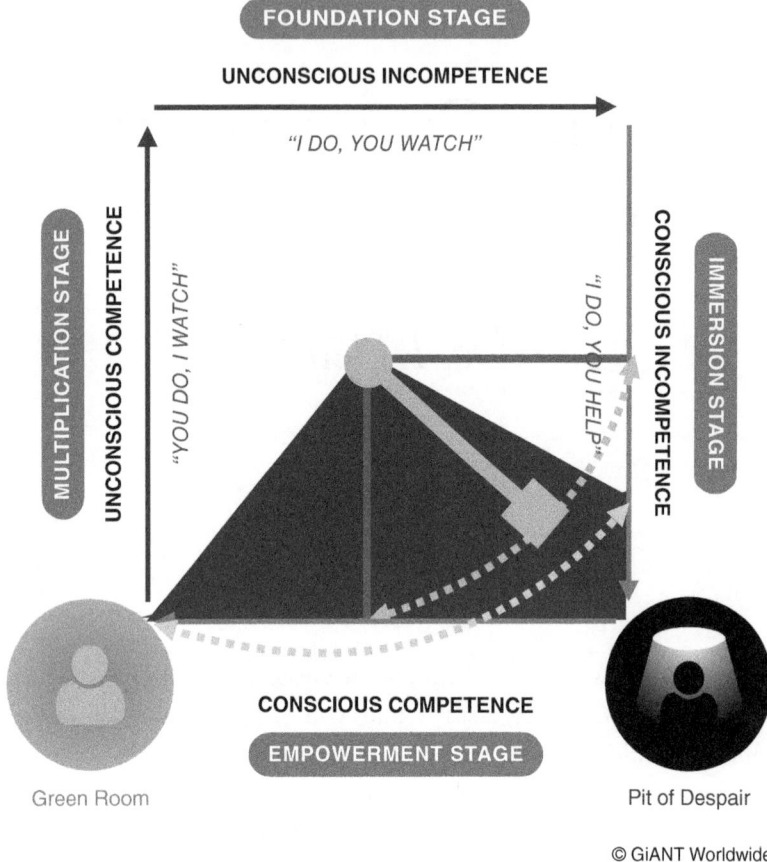

Source Credit: A. Maslow, Gordon Training International

Figure 9.1   The Empowerment Stage

abandon their people, while team members navigate the uncomfortable pendulum swing between confidence and uncertainty as they build consistent competence.

Team members' success in this stage requires calibrated support, structured feedback, and intentional encouragement over a longer period than most leaders anticipate. When executed effectively, the Empowerment Stage creates confident, capable leaders who can function without constant oversight, setting the foundation for true leadership multiplication.

The Long, Hard Road to Competence

A leader stands at the edge of the room as a team member prepares to lead a client presentation for the first time. The leader has reviewed the slides. The message has been practiced. They've rehearsed tough questions. The leader nods silently as the meeting begins, fully aware that what happens next isn't left to chance.

This is the defining moment of the Empowerment Stage.

It's a critical shift—not just for the team member stepping forward but for the leader learning to step back. Until now, you've been guiding your team members through every move: modeling, explaining, correcting. You've helped them build competence. Now it's their turn to lead—and your role shifts from instructor to support.

But here's what most leaders miss: This transition doesn't happen by accident. Empowerment isn't about "seeing how they do" or hoping they rise to the occasion. It's about intentionally setting them up to succeed.

If their first experience at this stage feels like failure, they can spiral back into the Immersion Stage, questioning themselves and their readiness. That's why great leaders invest the time to prepare their people for this moment. Great leaders anticipate the pressure points, coach them through key challenges, and give them every tool they need to own the outcome.

Growth isn't always clean. There will still be missteps. But when the foundation is solid and the preparation is intentional, the Empowerment Stage becomes the most rewarding stage of development— both for the person stepping up and for the leader cheering from the sidelines.

The Hardest Part of Leadership Development

The Empowerment Stage is where real leadership development begins. It marks the shift from you doing the work to someone else owning it—with you coaching from alongside.

It's the move from "I do, you help" to "You do, I help."

The team member becomes the primary executor. You shift into a coaching role—close enough to guide, but not doing the work for them. Mistakes happen, and how you respond will either accelerate growth or stall it.

This stage requires consistent, calibrated leadership. It's a constant dance between support and challenge. If you offer:

- Too much support? They become dependent on you.
- Too little? They feel abandoned and lose confidence.

It's like teaching someone to ride a bike. You don't hold on forever, but you also don't shove them down the street and hope they figure it out. You run beside them—steadying when needed—while allowing them to feel the balance for themselves.

This is what leadership looks like in the Empowerment Stage.

You've built their foundation. You've walked them through real challenges. Now your role shifts again—not into absence but into intentional proximity. You're present but not controlling. You're ready to help, but only when they need it.

Leadership development is more art than science. You're managing not just performance but emotions, confidence, and countless unseen variables. Things outside of work—health, family, fear—can all show up in the Empowerment Stage. That's why the relational element becomes essential.

This is the phase where trust deepens and where true partnership forms. It's where the leader shifts from a directive voice to a coaching presence. Jesus modeled this beautifully when He said, "I no longer call you servants. . .I have called you friends." That transition—from authority to ally—is the essence of the Empowerment Stage.

When leaders embrace this shift, they unlock something profound: people who lead not just from competence but from confidence and connection. And that changes everything.

Empowerment isn't stepping back; it's supporting someone well in the role you hired them to do.

Why Building Consistency Takes So Long

The goal of the Empowerment Stage is to help people reach Conscious Competence—where they not only understand what they're doing but can consistently execute it with confidence. But getting there? It takes a lot longer than most leaders expect.

That's because the Empowerment Stage is where the pendulum starts to swing.

This isn't a smooth, straight-line journey. It's a pendulum arc—forward into confidence, then backward into uncertainty, then forward again. Early in this stage, your team member will experience moments of both Conscious Competence and Conscious Incompetence. That swing back and forth is normal. It's not regression; it's repetition.

Growth looks like:

- One win, followed by a step back.
- One confident delivery, one moment of doubt.
- A strong start followed by a hesitant finish.

That's how the pendulum moves. That's how mastery is built.

Why It Feels So Unstable

Here's what makes this stage especially challenging for both learners and leaders:

- Execution is harder than it looked. Watching you lead made it seem easy. Doing it themselves reveals the hidden complexity.

- Confidence is fragile. Early wins build momentum, but the first big mistake can feel like a setback rather than a step forward.
- Mistakes carry more weight. When learners were helping, errors felt like feedback. Now that they're owning the outcome, those same errors feel like failure.
- Your role has changed. You're not leading from the front anymore; you're guiding from alongside. Learners are on the field, but you're still responsible for the score.

And that last point is critical:

In the Empowerment Stage, you're still accountable. They're doing the work, but you are still responsible for the outcome. Multiplication happens in the next stage.

Most leaders underestimate how demanding this stage is—not just for their team but for themselves.

The biggest mistake? They get impatient.

- They assume someone is failing when they're actually still learning.
- They step back too early, expecting independence before it's earned.
- Or they step in too quickly, rescuing their team and short-circuiting the growth process.

The Empowerment Stage is deceptively time intensive. Many leaders feel they've already invested enough time getting someone around the Pit of Despair in the Immersion Stage, and they're surprised to learn that the Empowerment Stage requires even more effort from them.

The Empowerment Stage is where the real work of leadership happens. You're not just teaching tasks; you're preparing someone to carry responsibility. And that means:

- Creating safe spaces to rehearse and practice.
- Giving real-time, post-execution feedback.

- Processing mistakes and reinforcing learning.
- Staying engaged long after you'd rather be hands-off.

The truth is: The Empowerment Stage is where leadership gets personal. You become a coach, not a manager. A mentor, not a micromanager.

The Hidden Complexity of Leadership Development

To make things even more complex, most leaders aren't just coaching one person through one Development Square. They're developing multiple people, on multiple journeys, at the same time—each one at a different stage, each one with a different Voice.

That's why true leadership multiplication is so rare. It's not because it doesn't work; it's because it requires more understanding, time, and intentionality than most leaders are prepared to give. That is exactly why we are writing this book—to provide a field manual to learn how to do develop people well.

> *Mastery isn't built overnight. It's the result of thousands of small corrections over time.*

The Slow and Steady Journey of Empowerment

For Gwen, a senior operations manager, empowering Tom didn't go the way she expected.

Tom had been with the company for years. He knew the warehouse inside and out, delivered results consistently, and had earned the respect of his peers. When Gwen promoted him to supervisor, it felt like a slam dunk. He already had the technical skills. Or so she thought.

What Gwen quickly discovered was that knowing how to do the work and knowing how to lead others in the work are two very different things.

She assumed Tom was ready for the Empowerment Stage of the Development Square. But, in hindsight, she hadn't properly walked him through the earlier phases:

- In the Foundation Stage, she hadn't modeled enough leadership moments for him to observe.
- In the Immersion Stage, she hadn't given him structured reps or processed learning from the times he assisted her.

So when Gwen handed off full responsibility too soon, Tom wasn't truly ready. He was sliding into the Pit of Despair—struggling with the weight of Conscious Incompetence.

At first, he was enthusiastic but erratic:

- He avoided delegation and did everything himself.
- When plans fell apart, he panicked and reacted emotionally.
- He leaned heavily on Gwen, asking for answers instead of thinking independently.

It became clear that Gwen had withdrawn too early in the Empowerment Stage. She expected independence before it had been earned.

Six months in, she recognized the pattern: Tom hadn't failed; she had skipped the process.

So, Gwen reengaged Tom with a new strategy. Instead of offering solutions, she began asking development questions that put the responsibility back on him:

- "What do you think we should do?"
- "If I weren't here, what would your next move be?"
- "Where's the breakdown—and what could fix it?"

These weekly check-ins became their rhythm. Not about task management, but about leadership development. Tom resisted at first—he was used to being the expert, not the one being stretched. But over time, things began to shift:

- He took ownership of the team schedule and solved breakdowns proactively.
- He started coaching instead of micromanaging his team.
- He stayed composed under pressure, even when things didn't go to plan.

By month 18, Gwen could see real traction. By month 24, Tom was running the show—and Gwen wasn't in the weeds anymore.

"It took almost two years," she reflected. "But now Tom leads with confidence. And more important, he's developing others."

That's the slow and steady power of the Empowerment Stage when it's done well. Most leaders don't give it enough time. They assume Empowerment is a handoff—but it's really a season of guided ownership, built on structured reps, honest feedback, and steady encouragement.

Tom didn't become a leader the day he was promoted. He became a leader when Gwen slowed down, reengaged, and helped him build the competence and confidence to lead on his own.

The Development Square Journey

As a reminder, here is the Development Square Journey (Table 9.1), which describes the leadership development journey.

The Leader's Role in the Empowerment Stage

Leadership becomes an art in the Empowerment Stage. Your challenge is to calibrate your presence—to stay close enough to support but far enough to let them lead. Here's what doing that looks like.

Encourage Progress, Even When It's Slow

- Celebrate effort, not just outcomes. The win isn't perfection—it's progress.

Table 9.1   Development Square Journey

Stage	Dynamic	Leader's Role	Team Member's State
Foundation Stage	"I do, you watch"	Demonstrate, explain, model	Unconscious Incompetence
Immersion Stage	"I do, you help"	Guide, teach, provide feedback	Conscious Incompetence
Empowerment Stage	**"You do, I help"**	**Coach, support, encourage**	**Building Conscious Competence**
Multiplication Stage	"You do, I watch"	Observe, affirm, release	Moving toward Unconscious Competence

- Recognize small wins. Confidence builds in the micro-moments, especially during messy growth.
- Normalize setbacks. Say it out loud: "This part is supposed to be hard."

Key Insight: Growth is rarely linear. Encouragement is what keeps the pendulum swinging forward.

Conversation Starter: "I've been watching your growth with [specific responsibility], and I believe you're ready for the next step. I'd like to transition this project so that you're leading it, with me supporting you. How does that sound?"

Calibrate High Support and High Challenge

- **Be Available, But Don't Hover.** Your presence builds security—but your encouragement of independence builds confidence and ownership.

- **Ask Before You Advise.** Try "If I weren't available and you had to decide right now, what would you do—and why?"
- **Give Feedback, Not Fixes.** Guide their thinking, and let them find the solution.

Key Insight: Your goal isn't to make the decision—it's to build their capacity to think and act like a leader.

Conversation Starter: "As we make this transition, my role will change. Rather than directing the work, I'll be here as a resource when you need me. You'll be making the decisions, and I'll help you process them. What questions do you have about this new dynamic?"

Resist the Temptation to Take Back Control

- **When they say "Can you just do it?"—don't.** Redirect instead: "Walk me through how you'd approach it."
- **When things feel off track, pause.** Let them feel the tension, navigate it, and grow.
- **Step in only when the consequences matter.** If it's just not your way, let it play out.

Key Insight: Not every mistake needs a rescue. Some mistakes need reflection and redirection.

Conversation Starter: "Let's set up a regular check-in—not for me to control the work, but for us to reflect on what's working and where you might need support. Would [specific time] weekly work for you to debrief and plan?"

Define What Full Ownership Looks Like

- **Clarify Success.** Don't assume they know what "owning it" actually means.
- **Set Visible Milestones.** Give them targets that show growth is happening.
- **Name the Transition.** When they're ready, say it: "You're doing this. I'm just here to support you now."

Key Insight: Empowerment accelerates when people know what they're aiming for—and when they hear that you believe in them.

Conversation Starter: "It's normal to feel some uncertainty during this transition. What part of taking the lead on this makes you most nervous? Let's talk through how we'll handle that together."

Your job isn't to be needed. It's to build people who don't need you.

When you empower someone well, clearly giving them the authority with the responsibility, you're transferring belief, ownership, and trust. And in the process, you're growing too.

What Success Looks Like

Mike Rubbo was a director of operations at a company that ran an e-commerce warehouse. One of his team members, Roger, was being trained to become a supervisor. A critical part of the role was tracking team productivity using a spreadsheet that measured how many items each person picked per hour.

The spreadsheet wasn't overly complex, but it did take some time to learn how to use it well. As the training started, Roger immediately expressed frustration. He admitted he hadn't had much experience using computers in a business setting, and he didn't see the point of doing the tracking at all.

At first, Mike showed him how it worked by doing the process himself. Then Mike handed it over to Roger while Mike observed. Roger was slow and had a lot of questions, and his frustration mounted quickly. That's when Mike realized Roger wasn't just struggling with the skill; he lacked the vision behind the task.

So Mike reframed it for him.

"When we started tracking this," Mike explained, "our team averaged 38 items per hour. Since implementing this process, we've grown to over 50. That weekly one-hour task has translated into 13 extra hours of output per employee. This isn't busywork; it's the reason we're more efficient."

The system clicked for Roger. With the "why" in place for him, they kept going. At first, movement was slow and time-consuming. A task Mike could do in one hour now took them two. But over the next few weeks, Roger gradually picked up speed. His frustration began to fade, and momentum took over.

Eventually Roger didn't need Mike standing over his shoulder. Roger could handle the spreadsheet independently—slowly at first, then confidently. Mike's role shifted from trainer to coach. Mike moved from doing the work alongside him to simply reviewing Roger's results in a few minutes each week.

And here's the best part: Mike now had time to focus on higher-level priorities, and Roger had grown in confidence and capability. Mike was able to affirm what he was doing well and celebrate his progress with specific, meaningful encouragement. What once felt like a drain on Mike's time became a breakthrough for both of them.

All in, Mike spent about 13 hours working with Roger on this process. But in return, Mike gained back 52 hours per year—and, even more important, he helped a future leader grow into the role. Roger had mastered the spreadsheet. Now it was time to teach him how to coach others, spotting what they were doing well and where they could improve.

Mike had taken Roger through the Foundation and Immersion Stages and guided him around the Pit of Despair by providing Time, Vision, and Encouragement, so that Roger could become Consciously Competent.

This is what success looks like.

When the Empowerment Stage is working, you'll feel it—and so will the people you are developing.

They will notice more confidence, more initiative, and more ownership in themselves. They will bring ideas, act, and recover quickly when things don't go as planned.

But if these things aren't happening, it's likely a sign that you're either still doing too much or not providing enough structure.

Here's how to self-check:

- If the individual still runs every decision through you, you're too hands-on.
- If projects are drifting without correction, you're too hands-off.
- If growth is inconsistent, you're likely not providing the right support.

True empowerment means you're needed less—and that's the point.

You haven't abandoned your teammates. It means they've grown to a point where they can lead without constant oversight. And that kind of ownership doesn't just lighten your load; it multiplies your influence.

The Cost of Avoiding Empowerment

When leaders sidestep the Empowerment Stage, the effects don't just impact one person; they compound across the whole team.

Some of the results that occur when leaders avoid the Empowerment Stage are discussed next.

Employees Stay Dependent

When leaders hesitate to truly empower, their people never develop beyond the tasks they're given. It's not because they're incapable; it's because they've never had the space to grow.

They wait for direction rather than thinking for themselves. They hesitate to act without approval. They become passive, even if they're performing the task well.

Over time, dependency doesn't just limit initiative; it limits capacity. The team becomes reliable executors but not self-directed contributors. They follow instructions but never fully own outcomes.

High Performers Quietly Stagnate (or Leave)

Some of your team will thrive under clear direction—but your high-capacity people won't stay in neutral for long. They want to stretch.

They want to grow. And if they don't see the opportunity to do so, they either disengage or walk away.

They get bored, even if they're busy. They plateau, even if they're productive. They leave, not because of the role but because they've outgrown the environment.

You Become the Bottleneck

If your team can't move forward without you, you're not scaling your leadership; you're bottlenecking the business. When leaders avoid empowerment:

- They stay buried in execution.
- They make decisions others should own.
- They create an invisible ceiling on team potential.

Even well-meaning leaders often mistake involvement for leadership. But if everything runs through you, your team's speed and scale will always be capped.

The Ripple Effect on the Team

Leadership development happens one person at a time, but the collective impact is massive. Empowered individuals bring sharper thinking, faster problem solving, and greater ownership to every interaction. When you invest in each person's growth, the culture shifts—and the team starts carrying the weight together.

You'll see:

- Initiative without prompting.
- Ownership without being told.
- Leaders who step up, even when you're not there to guide them.

Why Some Leaders Struggle with Empowerment

Empowering others sounds simple—until you try it. Many leaders hit a wall in this stage because it forces them to change how they lead.

They must shift from being the driver to becoming the coach. That's uncomfortable. It feels inefficient. And it's tempting to either take back control or check out altogether.

Here are three common traps leaders fall into—and how to overcome them.

1. The "I-Can't-Let-Go" Problem

Some leaders—especially Guardians, Creative/Pioneers, and Pioneers—struggle to hand over real responsibility. They believe:

- No one can do it as well as I can.
- If they fail, it reflects poorly on me.
- It's faster if I just do it myself.

The problem? When you hold on too tightly, your team never grows. You may get short-term results, but you'll be the bottleneck in the long run.

David, a Guardian leading a finance team, had a capable manager ready to take over budgeting. But every time a report was due, David rechecked every number, edited the work, and reworked decisions. Over time, the manager stopped offering ideas, knowing David would override them anyway.

David thought he was protecting quality. Instead, he was blocking development.

Empowerment takes trust. If you always step in, your team won't step up. Let go of perfection so people can learn through real responsibility.

2. The "I-Let-Go-Too-Soon" Problem

Other leaders trust quickly and hand off ownership before their team is fully ready. They assume enthusiasm equals preparedness.

They say things like:

- "You've got this!"
- "I trust you to figure it out."
- "Let me know if you run into trouble."

Although good intentions are there, team members can be left feeling unsupported and overwhelmed.

Lisa, a Connector running a nonprofit, gave a junior manager full control of a major fundraising event. She believed in him and loved his passion—but skipped the planning and coaching phase. Without structure, the manager missed key details, and the event nearly fell apart.

Lisa didn't set him up to fail, but she didn't set him up to succeed either.

Empowerment doesn't mean disappearing. It means giving ownership with clear guardrails and consistent connection.

3. The "I'll-Save-You" Problem

Some leaders—especially Nurturers—struggle to let others feel the discomfort of challenge. They step in too early, thinking they're being helpful, but they actually interrupt growth.

You'll hear:

- "I could tell they were struggling, so I just took over."
- "I didn't want them to be embarrassed."
- "I figured I'd just get it done to save them the stress."

Stephanie, a Nurturer, gave a team member the chance to present to a key client. But sensing his nerves, she jumped in midmeeting to "help." She meant well—but it unintentionally signaled that she didn't believe in him. Over time, that team member stopped volunteering to lead.

Growth requires struggle. If you're always rescuing people from hard moments, you're also robbing them of the confidence that comes from overcoming.

The Empowerment Troubleshooting Guide

Even with the best intentions, leaders often encounter specific challenges during the Empowerment Stage. When you notice the warning signs shown on the next table, use the listed approaches to get back on track.

Table 9.2   Empowerment Troubleshooting Guide

Challenge	Signs It's Happening	Solution Approach
Premature handoff	Team member seems overwhelmed, asks basic questions, or work quality drops dramatically.	Step back into more structured coaching. Reestablish clearer parameters and more frequent check-ins. Say: "Let's break this down into smaller pieces."
Micro management	You find yourself rewriting their work, correcting minor details, or taking back tasks.	Pause before intervening. Ask yourself: "Is this a learning moment or a control issue?" Schedule feedback sessions instead of real-time corrections.
Confidence drops	After initial progress, team member becomes hesitant, seeks excessive approval, or stops taking initiative.	Celebrate specific wins. Normalize setbacks: "This is exactly where growth happens." Provide targeted encouragement around their strengths.
Unspoken expectations	Frustration builds because you expected something different from what was delivered.	Revisit and document clear success criteria. Ask: "What does excellence look like for this project?" Create alignment before execution.
Skill versus will gap	Uncertain if the issue is capability or motivation.	Have a direct conversation: "I notice [specific behavior]. Help me understand if this is a matter of needed training or priority." Adjust your approach based on the answer.

Remember that troubleshooting these issues early prevents the team member from slipping back into the Immersion Stage and maintains the momentum you've worked so hard to build.

> *Empowering others requires leaders to let go of what feels easy and embrace what builds others.*

How Each Leader Approaches Empowerment by Voice

Every leader wants to empower others, but not all approach it the same way. Your Voice influences how you lead through the Empowerment Stage—both your strengths and your blind spots. Some leaders struggle to release control. Others delegate too quickly and disappear.

Next, we discuss how each leader typically engages in the Empowerment Stage via the 5 Voices—and what to watch out for.

Voice-Driven Empowerment: How Each Voice Navigates the Challenge of Releasing Control

Every Voice has a superpower—but that superpower comes with a shadow. In the Empowerment Stage, leaders are no longer driving the work themselves. They're guiding others who are now doing it. This is the most critical—and often the most difficult—transition in development. And how a leader shows up in this stage is often determined by their foundational Voice.

Let's take a deeper look at how each Voice naturally empowers others—and where they're most likely to struggle.

Nurturer

Strength: Encourages growth with empathy and support
Common Mistake: Steps in too soon to protect from discomfort

Nurturers are the emotional anchors of teams. They create environments of safety, support, and trust—ideal conditions for growth. But when they see a team member struggling, their instinct is often to jump in and fix it. They feel the emotional weight of others' discomfort and interpret that tension as a problem to solve rather than a necessary step in the learning process.

What's often hidden underneath is self-doubt. Many Nurturers wonder: Why would someone want to learn from me? Am I really worth following? That imposter syndrome causes them to hesitate when the moment calls for challenge or release.

Adjustment Needed: Believe that your consistency is enough. Your presence provides safety even when you're not solving the problem. Let the person you're developing feel the tension of learning something new. That discomfort is not a threat—it's the path to confidence.

Creative

Strength: Inspires with vision and possibility
Common Mistake: Struggles with clarity, structure, and timing of release

Creatives see what others don't. They envision future possibilities and help others believe in what could be. But in the Empowerment Stage, inspiration alone isn't enough. Creatives often assume others "get it" because it makes so much sense in their own minds. They may pass off responsibility without enough clarity—or release too early before the person is truly ready.

Adjustment Needed: Ground your vision in practical steps. Walk learners through what good execution looks like. Don't just give the destination; map out the road. You'll build far more confidence (and fewer do-overs) when you combine inspiration with structure.

Guardian

Strength: Provides consistency, process, and accountability
Common Mistake: Holds on too tightly and struggles to fully empower

Guardians are wired for responsibility. They ensure things are done the right way and are fiercely protective of quality. But that same wiring can keep them from releasing ownership. Even after handing something off, they may micromanage or second-guess, sending the message: I don't trust you yet.

Adjustment Needed: Reframe your role. You're not auditing a process; you're developing people. They need space to apply what you've taught, even if it looks different from how you would do it. Instead of asking "Did they do it perfectly?" ask "Did they learn how to think like a leader?"

Connector

Strength: Builds belief and motivation in others
Common Mistake: Delegates too quickly and overlooks follow-through

Connectors are natural encouragers. They're masters of buy-in and can make people feel like they can take on anything. But in the Empowerment Stage, belief must be matched with structure. Connectors often hand off responsibility too soon, assuming someone is ready just because they said "yes."

Adjustment Needed: Check for understanding, not just enthusiasm. People don't always know what they've signed up for. Your relational connection builds trust, but your consistency builds ownership. Stay close enough to guide the execution, not just the energy.

Pioneer

Strength: Pushes people toward growth and high performance
Common Mistake: Expects too much, too soon

Pioneers are wired for challenge. They want people to grow, fast—and they often believe struggle is the best teacher. Although that's partially true, Pioneers can push so hard that team members lose confidence before they ever gain traction. Without enough support, people experience pressure instead of progress.

Adjustment Needed: Pace the challenge. What feels like a stretch to you may feel like a cliff to someone else. Break large responsibilities into smaller phases, and give just enough feedback to spark learning without micromanaging. You'll still drive results—but with far less burnout.

No Voice Is Naturally Great at Every Stage

Some leaders step in too much. Others disappear too soon. The best leaders calibrate, adjusting their tendencies to meet the needs of the person they're developing.

If you want to be effective as a leader, you have to understand that leadership development is Voice-Driven. It's not one-size-fits-all. It's one Voice, one stage, one challenge at a time.

Empowerment Is the Heart of a Liberation Culture

Empowerment isn't a nice-to-have; it's the engine of every thriving, scalable team. At GiANT, we call this kind of environment a Liberation Culture—a culture where leaders don't just manage outcomes, they build people. It's where freedom and responsibility go hand in hand and where the goal is not just efficiency but transformation.

Liberation happens when leaders stop holding all the reins and start equipping others to lead. It's the shift from control to trust, from directing work to developing leaders. In a Liberation Culture, empowerment isn't optional; it's essential.

Empowerment Versus Overpowering

Here's the hard truth: If you're still making every decision, solving every problem, and holding all the responsibility, you're not empowering, you're overpowering.

- Overpowering is doing others' work so you can stay in control.
- Empowering is equipping others to do work themselves for the good of the team.

Overpowering leaders build dependence. Empowering leaders build capability.

The best leaders don't just assign; they transfer ownership. They don't just delegate; they develop. That's the difference.

Empowerment Isn't Abdication

Let's be clear: Empowerment doesn't mean disappearing. It's not "sink or swim." That's abdication.

Real empowerment means giving people both the opportunity and the tools to succeed. It looks like:

- Clear expectations
- Guardrails for growth
- Consistent coaching
- Timely encouragement

The real test of leadership is what your people can do without you in the room.

It's a partnership built on trust—and when it's done well, it leads to ownership, maturity, and momentum.

The Prize Must Be Worth the Price

Empowerment is hard. It takes time, energy, and emotional investment. It's slower than you want. Messier than you expect. More demanding than you think.

But it's also more rewarding than anything else in leadership.

Most leaders hesitate to pay the price because they don't fully understand the prize. But here's what's waiting on the other side:

- A team that doesn't need constant oversight
- Employees who take initiative, own outcomes, and solve problems without you
- A culture that builds leaders from within—again and again

That's not just a win. That's a winning culture.

Reflection Questions

As you prepare to implement the Empowerment Stage with your team, take time to reflect on these questions:

- Which team members are ready for more responsibility, and which responsibilities am I still holding that should be transferred?
- When was the last time I stepped in to "rescue" a situation? Was it truly necessary, or was I responding to my own discomfort?
- How does my Voice influence my approach to empowerment? What specific adjustments do I need to make to better support my team's growth?
- Am I providing enough structured feedback, or am I assuming my team knows what I'm thinking?
- What's my biggest fear about fully empowering my team members? How might that fear be limiting their growth?
- When was the last time I celebrated progress rather than just outcomes? How might I better acknowledge the growth journey?
- How long am I willing to invest in this stage before expecting consistent results? Am I being realistic about the timeline?

Leader's Challenge: Are You Ready to Let Go?

Here are five steps you can take to lead your people more effectively:

1. Identify one team member ready to be empowered.
   Ask yourself: "Who has potential but needs intentional support to step into full ownership?"
2. Pinpoint where they are on the Development Square.
   Are they still watching? Helping? Starting to lead? Knowing their location shapes how you coach them.
3. Hand off a real responsibility, not just a task.
   Make it meaningful. Set clear expectations. Stay available, but let them lead.

4. Coach instead of control.

> Ask more questions than you answer. Don't rescue. Stay present and patient.

5. Celebrate progress—even if it's messy.

> Recognize growth. Reinforce belief. Stay the course.

As team members develop consistency in the Empowerment Stage, you'll notice something profound happening. Their need for your active guidance diminishes. Their confidence solidifies. They begin solving problems with the same principles you've taught, but in their own unique way. When this happens consistently, you're approaching the final frontier of leadership development: the Multiplication Stage. In the next chapter, we explore how to recognize this transition and make the final shift from "You do, I help" to "You do, I watch"—completing the development journey and unlocking your team's full potential.

10 | The Multiplication Stage

"You Do, I Watch"

You pause in the doorway of a conference room, watching silently. Inside, one of your leaders is guiding the team through a critical decision. The leader is asking the questions you would ask and navigating conflict with the values you've championed. This leader is developing others in real time.

And you're not needed—not because you're irrelevant, but because you've succeeded.

This is the Multiplication Stage (see Figure 10.1)—the moment your leadership transcends your presence. They're not just executing. They're not just owning the outcome. They're leading with intention, casting vision, coaching others, and shaping culture. They've stepped into the next level—and they're taking others with them.

For most leaders, this moment never arrives.

They stall at the Empowerment Stage. They build performers, not multipliers.

STAGE FOUR: **MULTIPLICATION**

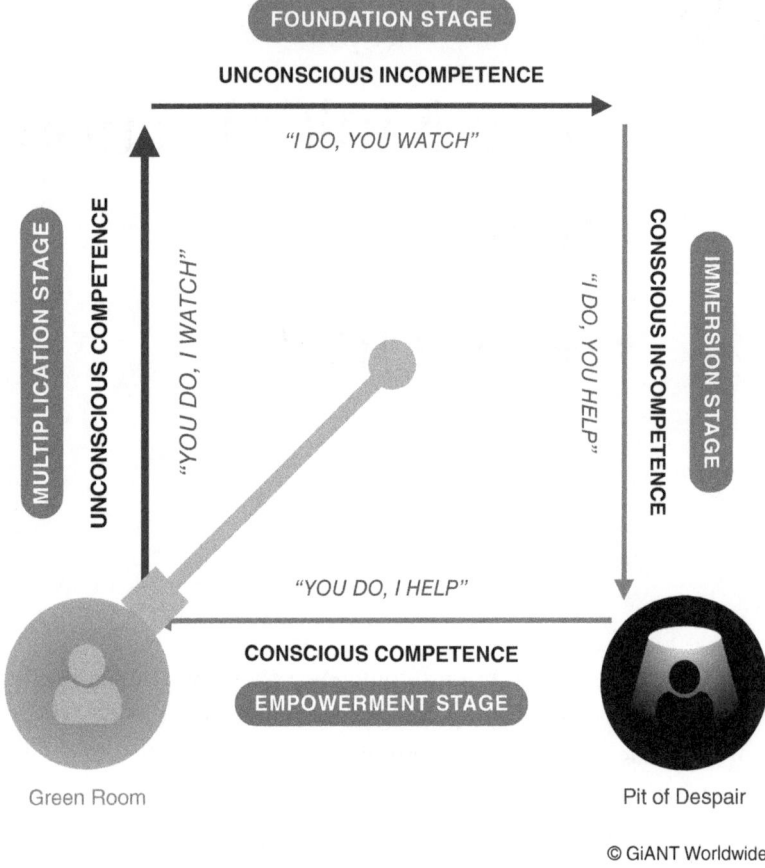

© GiANT Worldwide

Source Credit: A. Maslow, Gordon Training International

Figure 10.1   The Multiplication Stage

That's where the pipeline leaks. The organization plateaus. Future leadership evaporates.

Why? Because multiplication demands the courage to truly let go. It requires investing in someone who will eventually do what you do—likely better than you do it. That release isn't just organizational; it's personal. But it's also the hallmark of a leader who builds what lasts.

You haven't stepped away. You've stepped up—to a leadership that reproduces itself.

Because the job of a Voice-Driven leader isn't to fill one square. It's to multiply many.

While maintaining your own Development Square with some, you're always initiating new squares with others—identifying talent, building capacity, and constructing the future.

Like a master teacher whose legacy lives in generations of students, your influence extends far beyond your reach when you multiply leaders who multiply others.

That's the ultimate measure of leadership—not what you accomplish alone but what continues through those you've developed.

> *True leadership isn't measured by what you accomplish but by the leaders you develop who continue the work.*

From Empowerment to Multiplication: What's the Real Difference?

The transition from Empowerment to Multiplication might appear subtle, but it represents a fundamental shift in your leadership impact.

Empowerment builds competence. Multiplication builds continuity.

Most leaders settle for Empowerment, celebrating when someone can lead independently. But Multiplication takes leadership development to its proper conclusion—when the person you've developed begins developing others, without your oversight, creating their own leadership pipeline.

The next table shows the distinction between Empowerment and Multiplication.

Empowerment is when someone becomes capable of executing consistently at a high level within your team.

Multiplication is when they take that capability into their own leadership domain, apply it successfully, and begin developing others through the same process.

Table 10.1   The Distinction Between Empowerment and Multiplication

Empowerment	Multiplication
You Do, I Help	**You Do, I Watch**
Focus: Building conscious competence in a specific role	**Focus:** Reproducing leadership DNA in new contexts
They execute with confidence—with your guidance.	They execute independently—in their own domain.
You remain ultimately responsible.	They own outcomes completely.
Success = Role mastery	**Success =** Leadership reproduction
Your job: Coaching toward proficiency	**Your job:** Mentoring toward independence
They lead the work.	They lead others doing the work.

Empowerment builds competence. Multiplication builds capacity.

It's a graduation of sorts—not just in skill but in identity.

They've moved from team contributor to team builder.

This stage is the tipping point in your leadership Development Square. You're moving from building a solid team to building a leadership bench. And doing that requires a mindset shift.

Many leaders stop short at Empowerment. They feel a sense of relief when someone no longer needs them for the daily grind. But Multiplication challenges you to go one step further—to make sure leadership continues long after you're gone.

You're not just equipping people to do the work. You're equipping them to replicate the leadership culture you've created.

That's the mark of a multiplying leader.

You've completed the foundational work of training, coaching, and empowering. Now your role shifts to that of cultural architect and leadership mentor. You establish the environment, model the values, and shape the development ecosystem—but the execution happens without your direct involvement.

If Empowerment is earning a driver's license, Multiplication is becoming a certified driving instructor who creates other instructors.

The Green Room: Where Growth Gets Comfortable

The Green Room represents the most deceptive phase in the development journey. It's a resting spot, the space between Empowerment and true Multiplication that can quickly become a leadership trap.

Just as a performer waits in the Green Room before taking the stage, team members who've achieved competency and confidence can linger here too long. They've mastered the role. They feel trusted. They're no longer in survival mode. But instead of stepping into Multiplication—developing others or new skills—they start to enjoy the spotlight. They like being the favorite. They start to feel a little. . .over secure.

They've stopped pushing boundaries and started defending territory.

Often leaders unintentionally reinforce this pattern. They trust this person implicitly. The relationship works smoothly. And rather than challenging the person to multiply, leaders continue assigning more responsibility—without raising the bar of leadership reproduction.

Here is what an employee in the Green Room looks like.

- High-performance execution with minimal initiative to develop others
- Subtle ownership mentality ("I've earned this position")
- Reluctance to share knowledge or distribute control
- Resistance to investing time in others' development
- Comfort with being the "go-to" person

Why It Matters. The Green Room feels good—for a while. But if people stay there too long, they stall their own growth and stunt the growth of others. Multiplication doesn't happen. Team capacity flattens. And the leader ends up with a strong performer who's no longer growing and not helping others grow either.

Here is how each Voice experiences the Green Room:

- **Nurturers** may settle into being go-to helpers, avoiding the discomfort of challenging others.
- **Creatives** might stay in the idea zone, hesitant to release their work or mentor practically.
- **Guardians** often get stuck in ownership—reluctant to trust others with their systems.
- **Connectors** enjoy the influence but may avoid the tough relational conversations required to lead others.
- **Pioneers** can grow proud of their success and resist the slower process of bringing others along.

Here is your role in helping the team member in the Green Room:

1. **Name It.** Help them see where they are. Say "You've earned trust, but now it's time to give it away. Are you ready to multiply?"
2. **Raise the Vision.** Recast the goal: not just to be great at your job but to make others great at theirs.
3. **Create Stretch Assignments.** Assign mentoring or development tasks that require them to invest in others.
4. **Shift the Metrics.** Begin evaluating them not just on what they deliver but on whom they're developing.

Here is what leaders shouldn't do with those in the Green Room:

- Don't keep piling on responsibilities without changing the expectations.
- Don't reward competence without challenging comfort.
- Don't confuse loyalty with growth; being dependable isn't the same as multiplying.

The Goal. Help people make the decision to leave the Green Room. The door is open—but they have to choose to walk through it.

Your job is to challenge them with belief, not pressure. If they rise to it, they become more than a strong team member—they become a multiplying leader.

Signs they're moving out of the Green Room include these:

- They initiate development conversations with peers or juniors.
- They begin delegating with intentionality—not just tasking but teaching.
- They ask for guidance on how to grow others, not just themselves.
- They begin to take ownership of culture, not just execution.

Recognizing When Learners Are Ready for Multiplication. One of the most common questions leaders ask at this stage is: "How do I know when it's time to fully release them?"

It's a legitimate concern. Premature release can create chaos. But delayed release stifles growth and limits organizational potential.

Multiplication isn't triggered by exceptional individual performance; it happens when someone demonstrates readiness to develop others systematically. The challenge is that by the conclusion of Empowerment, this person typically has become one of your most reliable, valuable team members.

That's where many leaders hesitate, lingering in the Green Room.

It's comfortable. It's productive. Your empowered team member is delivering results, meeting targets, and making your leadership look effective. Why risk changing that dynamic?

But the Green Room quickly becomes a liability.

If you don't invite your highest performers into Multiplication, they'll inevitably:

- Develop an inflated sense of importance or become perceived as favorites.
- Become complacent in roles they've mastered.
- Miss the transformative experience of guiding others through the Development Square.

Here are the clear indicators they're prepared for the bottom-left corner of their own Development Square—the starting point for Multiplication:

- They make strategic decisions confidently without seeking your validation.
- They anticipate and resolve problems before escalation.
- They claim full responsibility, especially when things don't go as planned.
- They naturally coach teammates without directive.
- They reflect meaningfully on their own development journey.
- They have established trust with others who already look to them for leadership.

If you remain the primary thinker, decision maker, and director, they're not ready. But if they've organically become leader's others gravitate toward—without your prompting? They're prepared for Multiplication.

> *Multiplication begins when your people build what you once had to lead.*

Your role now is to help them cross this crucial threshold: out of the Green Room and into leading others through their own Development Square.

Most leaders stop too soon, settling for competence instead of investing in continuity.

But high-capacity cultures don't just celebrate achievement; they replicate leadership.

Why Some Leaders Struggle to Multiply

Stepping into the Multiplication Stage sounds exciting in theory, but, in practice, it can be one of the most uncomfortable shifts a leader will ever make.

You've spent years being the go-to person. Now you're being asked to step back and watch others do the things you once owned.

Even when your team is ready, letting go can trigger a whole range of internal resistance.

Next, we discuss two of the most common struggles.

The I-Still-Want-to-Step-In Problem

This problem shows up when leaders feel compelled to stay involved, even after their team member has demonstrated readiness.

- "If I step back completely, things might fall apart."
- "I still have valuable insight; I should keep contributing."
- "If they mess up, it reflects on me."

Bill, a Guardian, led a well-oiled operations team. He had spent nearly two years developing his manager, who had grown into a thoughtful, strategic, and highly capable leader. She had earned the right to lead independently. But every time a key decision surfaced, Bill still weighed in—offering advice, adjusting plans, or subtly over-ruling her decisions.

What Bill didn't realize was that his manager was ready to enter the Multiplication Stage. But instead of crossing the thresh-old into Multiplication, she got stuck in the Green Room—a place of comfort, recognition, and familiar success. She was executing flawlessly but hadn't yet started her own Development Square with someone new.

Why? Because Bill hadn't released her fully.

He thought he was protecting the work.

What he was actually doing was capping her growth—and the team's.

Multiplication isn't just a promotion; it's a graduation. But to graduate, a leader must be allowed to own, lead, and begin developing others without the constant shadow of their mentor.

Leadership Insight. Micromanagement doesn't maintain high standards; it maintains dependency.

The If-I'm-Not-Needed, What's-My-Role? Problem

This problem concerns the emotional undercurrent few leaders talk about—and it shows up most often in Connectors and Pioneers who thrive on being in the center of the action.

- "If the team can run without me, what's my purpose now?"
- "I built this team—shouldn't I still be involved?"
- "If they don't need me anymore, am I still valuable?"

This question isn't a selfish one; it's a human one.

Ashley, a high-energy Connector, had poured years into building a strong strategic planning team. She empowered her people well, and one day, they ran a full offsite without asking for her input. It was a sign of success—textbook Multiplication Stage.

But Ashley didn't feel proud. She felt. . .lost.

She wasn't sure where she fit anymore. Her team was flying—and she felt like she was back at square one, rebuilding with a brand-new group.

That's the quiet cost of true multiplication. You don't just let go of tasks; you let go of people. You release them to rise, to lead others, to build their own teams—and that means returning to the earlier stages of development with someone new.

It's not glamorous. It doesn't always feel rewarding. And yes, you may miss the team you have developed. But that's the point.

The Green Room is the uncomfortable moment when a leader is ready to rise. . .and the developing leader must choose whether to release them or keep them close for comfort. Many leaders hesitate here, not because they don't believe in the person but because they're not ready to give up the familiarity, success, or relational gratitude they've grown used to.

But here's the truth: If you never feel this tension, you're probably not multiplying.

Multiplication isn't a loss; it's legacy.

It means doing the hard work again. It means choosing the long game over comfort. And it means reminding yourself that your value isn't tied to being in the room; it's measured by who rises when you're not there.

Multiplication challenges your need to be the hero.

It invites you to become the architect of something far bigger than yourself.

> *If your individual members can't thrive without you, you've built a cage, not a legacy.*

From Manager to Multiplier: The Story of a Vice President Who Finally Let Go

Phase 1: The Wake-Up Call

Noah was a vice president in a fast-growing company. Known for his work ethic and reliability, he had built a reputation as the go-to problem solver. Whether it was strategy, performance, or crisis, he could step in and get it done.

But as the business grew, so did the complexity—and the cracks began to show.

Noah had a strong leadership team on paper, but they weren't truly leading. His directors ran everything by him, deferred to his judgment, and paused when he was out of office. The team operated well—as long as Noah was present.

He thought he had empowered them.

In reality, he had created dependence.

Then came the text from his wife: "You missed Emma's recital. Again."

That night Noah asked himself the question that every overwhelmed leader eventually must face: "If I disappeared tomorrow, would this team know how to function without me?"

He knew the answer. And he didn't like it.

Phase 2: Owning His Own Development Square

Noah realized something hard: He had never actually learned to develop people.

He was effective at delegation—but delegation isn't development.
He had skipped straight to the Empowerment Stage.

Without investing time in the Foundation Stage or the Immersion Stage, his team never truly learned how to own their roles.

When they struggled, he jumped in—thinking he was helping, but actually short-circuiting their growth.

So Noah humbled himself.

He found a coach.

He studied the Development Square.

And, most important, he discovered the 5 Voices.

That was the breakthrough.

He realized that his own Pioneer Voice had driven his tendency to expect people to "just get it." He had unintentionally pushed at a pace most of his team couldn't sustain.

Grace, his director of ops, was a Guardian: structured, thoughtful, risk averse. She didn't need grand vision. She needed time, clarity, and feedback loops.

Luis, his sales lead, was a Connector: relational, optimistic, and great at influence. But he lacked the systems to develop others consistently.

Noah had been trying to develop them the way he liked to be developed.

Now he would learn to lead them the way they were wired.

Phase 3: Rebuilding

Noah sat down with each of his direct reports and mapped out a development plan for each of them.

No vague expectations. No "figure it out."

He identified the specific competencies they needed to master—and committed to walking them through the Development Square:

- In the Foundation Stage, he modeled how to do it.
- In Immersion Stage he let them help—coaching closely and correcting in real time.

- In Empowerment Stage, he gave them ownership but stayed present for support.
- And finally, he began to see signs of Multiplication—they were doing the work and developing others.

At times, it felt slower than just doing it himself. But the payoff was beginning to show.

Grace began leading strategy sessions with confidence. Luis started mentoring new hires with intentionality.

Phase 4: Multiplication Begins

The real shift came when Grace launched a development track for her own managers—without being asked.

She was creating her own Development Square. And Noah wasn't in the room. He wasn't driving it anymore. He wasn't even needed.

And that was the point. He didn't just develop leaders. He *multiplied* them.

- He didn't hand off tasks. he transferred trust.
- He didn't manage performance; he built capacity.
- He didn't just run a team; he helped shape a culture where leadership was scalable.

He had moved from being the engine to becoming the architect. From being the bottleneck to becoming the builder.

Noah didn't step back because he was tired. He stepped up—because his team was ready.

You don't build a leadership culture by running everything. You build it when the people you've developed start building others.

Multiplication Is the Ultimate Leadership Test

The Multiplication Stage isn't about doing more. It's about building something that outlasts you.

You'll know you've reached it when your name is no longer on every decision.

When your best people are leading meetings, you're not in.

When your joy comes not from being the hero but from watching those you developed build leaders of their own.

But here's the truth: Multiplication isn't just a leadership milestone; it's the ultimate test.

Because if the leadership pipeline ends with you, your impact ends with you.

But if it continues through others, your influence multiplies far beyond your role.

And yet this is also where development costs the most.

Multiplication requires real sacrifice—especially for team leaders who are still measured by short-term performance. Releasing your best people might mean a dip in output while you start the process again with someone new. It's risky. It's costly. And it works only if Multiplication is a shared value modeled from the top.

Here's the challenge: You've trained them. You've empowered them.

> *The true test of leadership isn't what happens while you're there—it's what continues when you're gone.*

Now it's time to release them—not because they no longer need you, but because they're ready to lead without you.

That's not a step back. It's the highest step forward.

The best leaders aren't remembered for what they built. They're remembered for who they built.

Here is your challenge as a leader working to Multiply your team.

1. **Identify Your Potential Multipliers.** Which team members show signs of readiness for Multiplication? Who is stuck in the Green Room?

2. **Create a Specific Multiplication Opportunity.** Select one leadership responsibility you currently own and deliberately transfer it to an emerging leader with this clear expectation: "I want you to lead this initiative completely and identify someone you'll develop through the process."

3. **Establish Multiplication Metrics.** Create specific measures beyond performance:
   - How many people are leaders actively developing?
   - Are they documenting their development process?
   - Are they adapting their approach to different Voices?

4. **Schedule a Multiplication Review.** Set a specific date to evaluate not just results but leadership reproduction. Ask: "Who is stronger because of your investment, and how are they now investing in others?"

5. **Celebrate Visible Multiplication.** Publicly recognize not just individual achievement but leadership reproduction. Make heroes of those who develop others, not just those who perform well themselves.

The more intentionally you multiply, the more enduring your influence becomes—because you're developing leaders who will develop generations of leaders to come.

Building a Development System

11

How to Build a People Performance System

Leadership Development Isn't an Event—It's a System

Leadership is one of the most misunderstood and underleveraged assets in modern organizations. Too often, development is reduced to sporadic workshops, executive retreats, or the promotion of top performers without guidance.

But leadership doesn't happen by accident.

Real leadership development is intentional. It's a system.

A system that builds people, reinforces culture, and multiplies trust and performance across every team.

Most companies don't need more content—they need a process. A pathway. A way to develop leaders consistently, not chaotically. And especially, a way to equip team leaders with what they need most: structure, clarity, and confidence.

The Problem Most Organizations Face

Most companies are still accidental in developing the most pivotal role in their business—the team leader.

Without a system:

- Communication breaks down.
- Trust erodes.
- Growth slows.
- Turnover rises.
- High performers burn out.

The result is that team leaders become bottlenecks instead of bridges. That's not a people issue—it's a system issue.

> The growth and development of people is the highest calling of leadership.
>
> —*Harvey S. Firestone*

Voice-Driven Development: Key Components

The 5 Voices People Development System transforms traditional human resources (HR) components into powerful culture-building tools. The next Voice-Driven component chart breaks down traditional approaches and the 5 Voices enhancements.

Introducing the 5 Voices Performance System

The 5 Voices Performance System is a scalable, intelligent framework that helps organizations develop healthy, high-performing team leaders who build others. It builds on the components in table below to create a well-rounded system to drive higher performance inside organizations.

It's built around three simple, powerful components:

1. **The Lens.** Self-awareness through the 5 Voices
2. **The Map.** The Development Square to track growth
3. **The Toolkit.** Leadership tools for communication, feedback, and development

Table 11.1 Voice-Driven Component Chart

Component	Traditional Approach	5 Voices Enhancement
Needs assessment	Generic skill gap analysis	Voice-specific strengths and blind spots with Development Square mapping
Training	One-size-fits-all workshops	Voice-tailored development experiences aligned to Development Square stages
Performance management	Annual reviews and ratings	Voice-based coaching and Development Square progression tracking
Succession planning	Subjective high-potential identification	Voice diversity and Development Square progression metrics
Mentoring & coaching	Random pairing or availability based	Complementary Voice pairings with Development Square stage guidance
Measuring impact	Training satisfaction surveys	Voice health metrics and Development Square progression analytics

Together, they form a system that:

■ Clarifies expectations.
■ Aligns language across teams.
■ Tracks growth through predictable stages.
■ Builds cultures where leaders multiply leadership.

This is not episodic training. This is a system that transforms team leaders into performance multipliers.

The Core Elements of the System

The 5 Voices

The 5 Voices are a practical framework that helps individuals understand their leadership style, tendencies, and impact. The framework enables leaders to communicate more effectively and collaborate with empathy and influence.

The Development Square

The Development Square is a visual roadmap that shows how people grow—from Foundation to Immersion, then Empowerment, and finally Multiplication. It helps team leaders assess where people are and coach them forward with clarity.

100X Tools

These visual tools are mirrors that leaders use to help develop people around personal growth, relational dynamics, and professional mastery with the goal of getting to 100% health and learning how to multiply.

All together, these frameworks power the **5 Voices Performance System**—a system that develops leaders at scale.

A Roadmap to Systemic People Development

No matter the size of your organization, the implementation pathway follows five foundational steps:

1. Individual Voice Discovery

- Every employee takes the 5 Voices Assessment.
- Leaders gain insight into their communication and leadership tendencies.

2. Team Voice Mapping

- Voice Maps show how teams are wired.
- Nemesis dynamics, Voice gaps, and balance issues become visible.

3. Facilitation Proficiency

- Leaders complete the 5 Voices Badge.
- HR and trainers earn certification to facilitate the system internally.

4. Integrated Leadership Development

- Teams use 5 Voices + Development Square in one-on-ones, meetings, and coaching.
- The 5 Voices Leader Academy helps high-potential leaders grow consistently.

5. Performance Tracking with OS Pro

- GiANT OS Pro uses 5 Voices AI to monitor Voice health, growth stages, and team dynamics.
- Development becomes measurable, not just meaningful.

Implementation Plans by Organization Size

Small Organizations (5–100 Employees)

- Start with 5 Voices Assessments.
- Team leaders complete the 5 Voices Badge.
- Launch Development Square conversations in one-on-ones.
- Use OS Pro to track growth and communication health.

Midsize Organizations (100–500 Employees)

- Roll out 5 Voices and Development Square company-wide.
- Certify HR and learning and development to facilitate and embed the system.
- Launch Voice-based leader development tracks.
- Monitor Voice health and pipeline progression quarterly.

Enterprise Organizations (500+ Employees)

- Conduct performance and leadership evaluations.
- Deploy 5 Voices AI via OS Pro to track development across departments.

- Integrate the Development Square into performance reviews.
- Use internal champions to drive Voice-led development at scale.

The Role of the 5 Voices AI

The upgraded **5 Voices AI** transforms the system into an intelligent engine for real-time coaching and cultural insight.

For Team Leaders
- [ ] Voice-based leadership prompts each week
- [ ] Suggested tools for team alignment, development, and communication
- [ ] Performance nudges based on team feedback

For Individual Contributors
- [ ] Personal growth prompts tied to their Voice
- [ ] Feedback, conflict resolution, and communication tips
- [ ] Weekly suggestions to improve influence

For HR and People Leaders
- [ ] Aggregate Voice data and trends
- [ ] Culture dashboards showing growth and gaps
- [ ] Role-based insights for team, leader, and org-wide development

Diagnostic: The Performance Assessment

The system begins with **two diagnostic tools:**

1. Performance + Leadership Assessment

Each team leader is rated by their leader from 1 to 10 in:

- **Performance:** Do they deliver results?
- **Leadership:** Do they develop people?

This helps prioritize development based on real-world impact.

2. *Team Voice Map*

Built automatically in OS Pro, this map identifies:

- Primary and secondary Voices
- Nemesis dynamics
- Underrepresented Voice types
- Common stress behaviors
- Team balance and communication styles

Together, these tools guide the next steps in each team's development journey.

Case Study: Hartford Homes—A Voice-Driven Development Culture

The Challenge: Hartford Homes, a $120M regional homebuilder, was scaling fast. Leadership was competent, but development was informal and inconsistent. Cross-team tension slowed down operations. High-potential talent had no clear development path.

The Approach: With the help of MOTiV, a consulting group and 5 Voices certified organization, Hartford implemented a Voice-Driven people system. Every team leader was trained in the 5 Voices and Development Square. Coaching and development became embedded in one on ones, onboarding, and team meetings. Here are examples of what they now do to develop their people.

- Onboarding now includes Voice + Square training.
- Managers coach using Voice-based feedback and square-stage support.

(continued)

(continued)

- Team leaders build their own leadership benches through intentional development.
- Cross-team friction dropped as alignment and trust increased.

The Result: Hartford didn't just grow; it multiplied.

- Execution bottlenecks disappeared.
- Managers became multipliers.
- Talent stayed—even in a down market.
- Culture became the competitive advantage.

MOTiV helped us unlock the efficiency of trust. The 5 Voices and Development Square gave us a system for consistent leadership development. Our people are more confident, aligned, and capable.

— Landon Hoover, CEO, Hartford Homes

The culture you want tomorrow is built by the leaders you develop today.

For organizations of any size, the next sequenced roadmap provides a clear path to implementation.

The Future of Leadership Is Systemic

The culture you want tomorrow is built by the team leaders you develop today.

The **5 Voices** Performance **System** gives you a complete, intelligent framework for turning accidental leaders into intentional developers of others.

If you can measure it, you can multiply it. If you can align it, you can scale it.

Leadership development isn't a perk—it's the lever that moves everything.

Begin with One Team

Don't wait for an all-company rollout; start with a pilot.

- **Choose One High-impact Team.** Select a department where improved leadership would make a significant difference.
- **Focus on One Competency.** Identify a core skill everyone needs to develop.
- **Apply the Development Square.** Map where each person stands (Foundation, Immersion, Empowerment, or Multiplication).
- **Lead Them Voice by Voice.** Use their foundational Voice of each team member to guide how you support and challenge them.

The culture you want tomorrow is built by the leaders you develop today. By implementing the 5 Voices People Development System, you're not just investing in training; you're creating a sustainable leadership multiplier that will transform your organization from the inside out.

When leadership development becomes the way your organization operates, that's when real transformation begins.

The 5 Voices System Resources

The following resources will help you explore the power of intentional Voice-Driven leadership.

5 Voices Assessment: This link gives you access to take the 5 Voices Assessment for free for you and for your teams or family members.

5 Voices Badge: This link leads to a 2.5-hour course for team leaders to become proficient in the 5 Voices so that they can lead their teams through the Development Square.

5 Voices Certification: This link leads to the 5 Voices certification for those who want to teach the 5 Voices internally or as a coach or a consultant.

Summary: Action Plan to Get Started

Whether you're an HR executive, team leader, or founder, this is your playbook:

1. **Start with Yourself.** Take the free 5 Voices Assessment.
2. **Map Your Team.** Use Voice maps to reveal team dynamics.
3. **Launch Development.** Equip leaders with the 5 Voices Badge and Development Square.
4. **Use OS Pro.** Monitor growth, track patterns, and receive weekly AI coaching prompts.
5. **Scale with Certification.** Build internal capacity with 5 Voices Certified Leaders.

You don't need to roll it out company-wide tomorrow. **Start with one team. One leader. One conversation.**

Conclusion

Are You Becoming a Voice-Driven Leader?

You've made it to the end of the playbook, but the real journey is just beginning.

By now, you know the truth: Leadership isn't just about driving performance; it's about unlocking potential. It's not about managing tasks; it's about multiplying people. And the leaders who do that best don't rely on one-size-fits-all approaches. They develop people based on how they're wired—Voice by Voice, skill by skill, stage by stage.

You've learned the frameworks. You've practiced the tools. Now comes the question that matters most:

Are you becoming a Voice-Driven leader?

Leadership Starts (and Grows) with Self-Awareness

Let's go back to where we started—with you.

We began this journey with a self-assessment. A mirror, not a report card. We took that approach because you can't take someone else through the Development Square until you've walked it yourself.

So now, after everything you've learned, it's time to reflect again—through a new lens.

Read the next paragraph slowly. Let it describe the leader you're becoming:

> As a team leader, I'm deeply committed to developing people the way they learn. I know my own leadership tendencies, and I adjust based on what each person needs in their stage of development. My team knows I am for them, not just for myself. I build trust, give feedback, and create space for others to grow—even when it's messy or slow. I know when to support, when to challenge, and when to get out of the way. I am clear on my expectations, vision, and how we can win. Our culture doesn't just produce results; it produces leaders.

Now pause and ask yourself:

- Am I making progress in my intention?
- Would my team see that I am becoming more effective as a leader?
- Would my boss agree?

What Do Your Numbers Reveal?

Take a moment to compare where you started and where you are now.

What changed? What grew? What's still developing?

These numbers don't define you; they *direct* you. They give you clarity on where to keep investing because Voice-Driven leadership is not a milestone. It's a mindset.

And your growth doesn't end here. This is your new normal:

- Reflect honestly.
- Adapt intentionally.
- Develop others intentionally.

Table C.1 Voice-Driven Leadership Assessment

Use the prompts to evaluate your current leadership approach.

Score each statement on a scale of 1 to 10, where:

10 = Fully true of me

1 = Not true at all

1. I am deeply committed to developing people according to their natural Voice. _____
2. I understand my own leadership tendencies and how they impact others. _____
3. I intentionally adjust my leadership style based on the needs and development stage of each individual. _____
4. My team knows that I care about their growth and development—not just about performance or results. _____
5. I actively build trust, provide meaningful feedback, and create space for others to grow. _____ _____ _____
6. I stay present and supportive even when growth is messy or slower than expected. _____
7. I can discern when to support, when to challenge, and when to step back to let others lead. _____
8. I communicate clear expectations and compelling vision and define what winning looks like. _____
9. I help create a culture that not only delivers results but develops Voice-Driven leaders. _____
10. I regularly seek feedback on my leadership from those above, beside, and below me to continually grow. _____

Your Final Challenge

You have the tools. You've learned the framework. You understand the power of Voice-based development.

Now it's time to *live it*.

Whether you're leading a team for the first time or leading the entire organization, remember: you are no longer a passive manager. You are a developer of people.

The culture you create tomorrow starts with how you lead today. Voice-Driven leadership is how transformation becomes tradition.

Let's go build leaders.

Acknowledgments

We are so grateful for our team. Each of you have worked so hard to create the systems to liberate so many. We love you all!

Thanks also to our partners in liberation around the world. From clients to coaches to partners and friends. Thank you for joining us in a movement that is far greater than brands. You all are amazing.

To our future clients, coaches, and friends, we are excited to get to know you and to partner with you in changing leadership culture, starting internally.

From Jeremie:
I want to personally thank my love, Kelly, our amazing daughters (Addison, Kate, and Bailey), and the son club (Will, Blake, and Brandon) for being consistently kind and constantly fun. I am more than grateful!

I also want to thank the Bulldog for his consistent friendship that has launched another season of impact.

From Steve:
To Becky, Stu, Jaz, Dan, and Graham, thank you for trusting me and allowing me to experience the joy of multiplication. Please forgive me for the times I got the calibration of support and challenge wrong!

About the Authors

Jeremie Kubicek and Steve Cockram are the cofounders of GiANT Worldwide, a global leadership company known for creating the *5 Voices*, one of the most powerful and practical tools for leadership, communication, and team performance in the world today. GiANT certifies coaches and equips organizations with a proven system to build confident leaders, cohesive teams, and healthy workplace cultures. With impact in over 100 countries—from Fortune 500 companies to fast-growing startups—GiANT is transforming the way people lead by helping them understand themselves and others more deeply than ever before.

Together Jeremie and Steve have written *The 5 Gears*, *The 5 Voices*, *The 100X Leader*, *The Communication Code*, and *The Voice-Driven Leader*.

Jeremie Kubicek is the *Wall Street Journal*–bestselling author of *Making Your Leadership Come Alive* and *The Peace Index* and coauthor of the classic leadership books listed above. Recognized by *Inc.* magazine as one of the Top 100 Leadership Speakers, Jeremie has been featured on MSNBC, *Entrepreneur*, *Inc.*, and inside some of the largest companies in the world.

As the CEO and cofounder of GiANT, Jeremie has built an ecosystem of brands designed to develop *liberating leaders* who transform teams, cultures, and entire organizations in every city and sector.

GiANT's global reach spans over 100 countries, helping leaders unlock their full potential through powerful frameworks—most notably the 5Voices.com, one of the most practical tools for self-awareness and team communication available today.

Jeremie speaks internationally, hosts the *GiANT Leadership Podcast*, and is passionate about creating content and traveling with friends. He and his wife, Kelly, have lived and led in Moscow, Atlanta, London, and now Oklahoma City. Together, they run The Farmstead, a family-owned event venue (FarmsteadVenue.com) and are the proud parents of three grown children—Addison, Will, and Kate.

Learn more at www.jeremiekubicek.com.

Steve Cockram is an inspirational communicator, serial entrepreneur, and confidant to elite leaders around the world. He is creator and coauthor of the 5 Voices communication system and cofounder of GiANT, a global leadership consultancy working in over 100 countries. His latest venture is called the Relationship Revolution.

Steve and his family have lived in on the moors of Yorkshire, the desert in Arizona, Pawleys Island in South Carolina, the hills of Devon, and now in West London. He and his wife, Helen, have three daughters—Izzy, Megan, and Charlie. He has a long-standing addiction to test match cricket, and Harewood Downs Golf Course is his spiritual home. He loves walking, watching movies, and eating long dinners with good friends. Find out more at www.stevecockram.com.

Index

OTHER BOOKS FROM
JEREMIE KUBICEK AND
STEVE COCKRAM

The Communication Code
ISBN: 978-1-394-15053-3

The Peace Index
ISBN: 978-1-119-98592-1

The 100X Leader
ISBN: 978-1-119-51944-7

The 5 Gears
ISBN: 978-1-119-11115-3

The 5 Voices
ISBN: 978-1-119-11109-2

The Voice-Driven Leader
ISBN: 978-1-394-15066-3